Keeping Faith at Work

The Christian in the Workplace

David A. Krueger

Abingdon Press
Nashville

KEEPING FAITH AT WORK: THE CHRISTIAN IN THE WORKPLACE

Copyright © 1994 by Abingdon Press

This book is printed on recycled, acid-free paper.

Library of Congress Cataloging-in-Publication Data

Krueger, David A.
    Keeping faith at work: the Christian in the workplace/David A. Krueger.
        p.   cm.
    ISBN 0-687-07053-8 (pbk.: alk. paper)
    1. Christian life.   2. Christian ethics.   3. Work (Theology)
4. Vocation.   I. Title.
BV4501.2.K74   1994
248.8'8—dc20   94-33706
                                                                                        CIP

Scripture quotations are from the New Revised Standard Version Bible. Copyright 1989 by the Division of Christian Education of the National Council of the Churches of Christ in the USA. Used by permission.

94 95 96 97 98 99 00 01 02 03 — 10 9 8 7 6 5 4 3 2 1

MANUFACTURED IN THE UNITED STATES OF AMERICA

CONTENTS

101065

ACKNOWLEDGMENTS

THIS BOOK IS A MODEST attempt to build bridges, between languages, communities, spheres of our lives. It draws upon many personal, intellectual, and professional influences without claiming profound expertise in any. From participation in vibrant churches which exuded life rather than death, such as Holy Trinity Lutheran Church in St. Louis, has come the personal knowledge that local congregations can be ongoing sources of spiritual renewal, educational provocation, and social vision that energize members to be faithful Christians in the world. From my teachers at the University of Chicago—James Gustafson, Franklin Gamwell, Robin Lovin—has come an appreciation for the richness of our theological and ethical traditions. Whatever clarity of thought the reader here finds is but a partial and imperfect glimpse of their influence. From my years at the Center for Ethics and Corporate Policy in Chicago, working with businesspersons, corporations, and congregations, has come an appreciation for the day-to-day struggles and challenges that arise in our efforts to put faith into practice in the workplace. I am grateful for persons such as B. J. Chakiris, Allan Cox, Davis Fisher, Ron Nahser, Mary Olson, and Art O'Neil, who live lives of creative vision and faithfulness and who have pushed me to make the language and concepts of my field intelligible and plain-spoken for the practitioner. I am also grateful to persons at Baldwin-Wallace College who have supported my intentions and efforts to do scholarship at a teaching institution, especially Neal Malicky, Mark Collier, Ron Ehresman, and Gene Beem.

Finally, I dedicate this book to Donald, enthusiastic pastor, and Marilyn, passionate educator, for whom the congregation has always been a vital place where faith transforms lives; and to Timothy and Alex, for whom I hope the congregation will still have relevance when they come to shape their identity as workers in the world.

David A. Krueger
Baldwin-Wallace College
Summer 1994

RELATING FAITH AND WORK: THE CHALLENGE FOR CHRISTIANS AND CONGREGATIONS

THIS BOOK SEEKS to help Christians at work. It aims primarily at the person in the pew who struggles with, celebrates, and ponders what it means to be a Christian in the workplace. As a book on applied Christian ethics, it probes the meaning and implications of our religious faith for how we act, value, make decisions, and organize our lives at work and in business. My primary audience is not professional theologians and ethicists, but laypersons in the world of business and other economic sectors who strive to be theologically literate so that they can live and work in ways consistent with their Christian faith.

Martin Luther's stress on Paul's biblical insight is crucial—we are justified by faith and not by works. Our work and actions within economic life do not save us. Nevertheless, relating our faith and our work is vital. If we renounce a compartmentalized faith that applies only to limited spheres of life—to what we do at church or to how we live with family and friends—then we must affirm the significance of our task at hand. Most adults spend more time at work than anywhere else, including time spent with families or at leisure. If we are to be Christians in the world, it will be in the workplace as much as anywhere else. One prominent ethicist, Max Stackhouse, suggests that the modern corporation has replaced the family as the most important social institution in the twentieth century.

We live in an age of rapid global change. Every generation makes this proverbial claim about itself and its world. Yet few would challenge its truth today. The peaceful collapse of the Soviet Empire will forever change global geopolitics. The cold war has ended. Former enemies are rapidly destroying their nuclear arsenals and drastically shrinking their conventional forces. Formerly totalitarian states grope hesitantly and unevenly toward forms of democratic pluralism. State-controlled economic systems awkwardly and painfully make themselves into market-based systems, not only in the former Soviet bloc but in the less-developed world as well. Global economic integration and rapid technological change disrupt and transform economic institutions and human lives within our country and throughout the world. Growing public consciousness and alarm about negative effects of human economic activity on the environment—global warming, the depletion of the ozone layer, rapid human population growth—suggest the need for continued, and perhaps radical, changes in the ways we live on planet earth. How should Christians respond to these changes profoundly affecting the world of work?

Closer to home, challenges within our work lives—personally and institutionally—require our Christian response. How to deal with an underperforming employee. How to cope with an unfair boss. How to motivate and inspire people. How to survive in a downsized organization requiring more and more from its employees. How to survive and confront sexual harassment and discrimination. How to exist in an organization whose corporate culture and values sometime conflict with our personal values and beliefs. How to decide whether to maintain domestic production and employment or move overseas. How to maintain integrity, honesty, and fair dealings with customers. How to juggle the never-ending myriad of constituent demands and interests competing for a manager's attention. Some moral issues in the workplace may seem easy to analyze and resolve in light of our Christian faith. Others do not. Some dilemmas may seem unsolvable. Some experiences and challenges can leave us perplexed, anxious, emotionally drained, confused, feeling powerless, enraged, or deeply wounded, or they can shake our faith in ourselves, in others, or in God.

What ethical values, norms, and resources from Scripture and our faith traditions should we use to ground our Christian identity and to shape our actions at work? What is the role of churches in shaping our Christian identity and Christian ethic at work? How can what we do as members of congregations shape what we do as participants within our work organizations? Can our faith make a difference for our work? Is there a Christian ethic applicable to work and economic life? If so, how can it help us confront and respond to some of the most critical issues facing persons in the workplace? What roles can congregations play in nurturing a vital connection between faith and work? We will wrestle with these questions in this book.

PURPOSES AND INTENDED AUDIENCES

This book is intended for educational use by religious groups, particularly within congregations. Examples include congregational study groups examining issues of faith and work; seminary courses such as Christian ethics, church and society, and pastoral care; and seminary-sponsored continuing education courses for laity. Each chapter concludes with study questions to stimulate discussion among participants. The approach is not narrowly denominational; it is applicable within all mainline Christian traditions. My theological orientation is pluralistic and broadly ecumenical, permitting readers and discussion groups to consider how the distinctiveness of their religious traditions will shape and enrich their vision and discernment of the relationships between faith and work. Recent studies indicate that theological traditions within North American Roman Catholicism, mainline Protestant denominations, and Judaism generate few real differences in how persons in the pew seem to relate their faith to their work. Hence, the theological and ecclesiological differences that divide people in other areas are not reflected so much in the ways members view their work and economic activity.

This book aims to attract laity especially but also clergy: laity who must relate the language and convictions of faith to their workplace roles and decisions, clergy who must pastor to and minister with those who are called to be Christians at work within the secular world. This book can bring clergy and laypersons together around a topic of mutual concern for discussion and reflection. Too often issues of faith and work are neglected within congregations. When these issues are discussed, they frequently uncover uncomfortable and sometimes seemingly insurmountable divisions between clergy and laypersons. Many businesspersons perceive their clergy either as *uninformed* about economic and business realities or, even worse, as *misinformed* about workplace realities. On the other hand, many clergy lament that their members from business and the professions often seem to lack basic literacy in the scriptural, theological, and moral language of religious traditions and communities to have a strong enough self-understanding of what it means to be a Christian in the workplace.

The unfortunate result of this literacy and experience gap between clergy and laypersons for congregations is typically twofold. First, congregations fail to act as communities of moral deliberation and mutual learning in which Christians openly probe all ethical issues of social life in light of their faith. Second, because of the general absence of such constructive conversation, congregations fail to reach their full potential as leaven in society, enabling church members to shape the character of institutional and economic life as effectively as they might. Rather than be the salt of the earth, we too often suffer the subtle, creeping, hard-to-diagnose disease of religious malaise in which our identity, values, and actions are more reflections of our materialistic, relatively affluent, consumer-oriented culture than they are of our Christian faith.

BRIEF OUTLINE OF CHAPTERS

In short, this book seeks to help you discern what it means to be a Christian in the workplace. It aims to identify ingredients for the construction of a Christian ethic for the workplace. Christian ethics is more than *content,* more than the transmission of ideas and concepts inherited from Scripture and tradition. It is also a vital *process* of reflection and deliberation among members of faith communities. This book is intended for use by groups within Christian communities of faith. This ethic implies an understanding of the church as a community of moral deliberation in which its members, both clergy and lay, share expertise and experience in a process of mutual learning, reflection, and discernment. The goal is to enhance not only the character of our life together as a faith community but also the capacity of church members to live faithfully as workers and participants in the economy.

Chapter 1 ("Faith and Economic Life: How Five Christians Make the Connections") offers five vignettes characterizing some of the typical ways that U.S. Christians, both clergy and laity, understand and live out a relationship between faith and work. These hypothetical persons represent various religious traditions, occupational and socioeconomic levels, and economic sectors within U.S. society. We will return to these characters throughout our discussions.

Chapter 2 ("The World of Work: How Things Look from Within") sets the stage for moral deliberation by discussing the world of work and economic life *from the inside out*. What are some prominent features of today's global economy? I describe some basic characteristics of contemporary economic life in its systemic, organizational, and managerial dimensions. I briefly identify some broad global trends profoundly affecting contemporary economic life and some general changes taking place within modern work organizations.

Chapter 3 ("Christian Ethics: Claiming the Vision and Language of Faith") discusses some fundamental theological and ethical themes of Scripture and various traditions of Christian ethics that can be elements of a Christian ethic for work. Because theological and ethical traditions in our churches are so diverse, I offer some basic norms and concepts that you might use to construct a Christian ethic at work, including divine sovereignty, stewardship, vocation, sin, grace, human dignity, love and justice, and ecology and the common good.

In chapter 4 ("Christian Ethics at Work: Translating Vision into Action"), I outline a process and a method of ethical discernment and judgment for work and economic life. This process involves consideration of several benchmarks to be factored into ethical judgments, conclusions, and strategies for action. They include the fact of complexity and change in modern economic life, the challenge of discerning the ethical relevance of Christian Scripture and theology for our work and lives today, the results-oriented nature of work and business, the discernment of the "more or less" of ethical action, the complexity of workplace roles and the ambiguity of power within organizations, and the need to view organizations as moral communities. Finally, I offer a hypothetical test case of a workforce reduction situation to illustrate a method of ethical discernment.

Chapter 5 ("Critical Issues for Christians at Work") briefly discusses five critical economic and workplace issues facing Christians and others as we move into the twenty-first century. These issues are (1) routine, professional integrity issues and challenges, (2) the changing relationships and expectations of organizations and their workers, (3) the persistence of discrimination and the challenge of diversity within the workplace, (4) the changing roles and responsibilities of governments in relation to the economy, and (5) the ecological challenge of environmental protection and sustainability.

Chapter 6 ("Strategies for Congregations") addresses the practical challenge of relating faith to work within the life and practice of the congregation—of doing Christian ethical reflection and shaping religious identity within the Christian community. I discuss some reasons why business and work tend to be neglected topics within the lives of congregations and some stumbling blocks to creating forms of ministry that more effectively help Christians connect their faith to their work. I propose a vision of the church as a community of moral deliberation and mutual learning, and I outline strategies, practical guidelines, and programmatic suggestions and resources for nurturing such activity within the congregation.

Chapter 7 ("Strategies for Christians at Work") moves beyond the walls of the gathered Christian community to consider how the individual Christian lives one's faith in the workplace. I discuss some reasons why ethics tends to be a neglected or difficult topic within the cultures of work organizations and some stumbling blocks to effective moral action. I urge that Christians wrestle with the question of the purpose of business in general and the purpose and mission of our work organizations. I also encourage you to create a personal Christian mission statement for work. Finally, I offer suggestions for strengthening an organization's ethical responsiveness as a means for putting faith to work.

CHAPTER ONE

Faith and Economic Life

How Five Christians Make the Connections

VIRTUALLY ALL CHRISTIANS in the work-place relate faith and work, explicitly or indirectly, with certainty or with doubt, passionately or lifelessly, with strong integration or with no integration. For some, faith and work are a seamless web, richly and creatively connected. For others, they seem like awkward fits or even contradictions, distant and miles apart. In his classic text *Christ and Culture,* the twentieth-century theologian H. Richard Niebuhr demonstrated how Christian thinkers from various faith traditions have radically differed in the ways they understand that Christian faith relates to life in society. Likewise, Christians differ dramatically in the ways they relate faith and economic life. Such differences can be due to a variety of factors: differences of theology, socioeconomic background, professional education and training, life experiences, political and economic convictions. These factors affect the judgments we make about economic systems such as capitalism and socialism, the role of government in economic and business life, the moral status of business organizations, the role of personal responsibility within work organizations, and the very purpose of work in our lives. There is no single definitive Christian way to relate faith to work and economic life.

The following five vignettes illustrate some typical ways that Christians, both clergy and laity, envision and live out a relationship between faith and work. These hypothetical persons represent different religious traditions, occupational and socioeconomic levels, and economic sectors within U.S. society. Their situations are meant to illustrate partially some ways that Christians in the United States relate their faith and their work. Some of your experiences and perspectives may be similar to theirs. And some of their situations may shed light for you in understanding persons whose experiences and perspectives may be very different from yours. Throughout the book, I will refer to these persons to show how they might shape Christian ethical responses to various workplace issues and challenges.

GEORGE BREMER

George Bremer is a fifty-nine-year-old senior vice president at the regional headquarters of Telemax, a large diversified U.S.-based multinational corporation, where he has been employed for twenty-five years. A loyal employee, George has seen the firm grow dramatically from a midsized company with domestic production and markets and a single product line into a global corporation with production facilities on four continents and product markets in nearly all countries across the globe. George is also a survivor, who has lived through the company's strong growth spurts and severe contractions, resulting in acquisitions and sell-offs of business units and, in the past decade, considerable workforce reductions, especially in high-priced labor markets such as the United States. To remain globally competitive, his company, like others, has moved significant domestic production abroad to lower-priced production sites.

George is a devout lifelong Episcopalian and has been a member of Grace Episcopal Church for twenty years, serving on its vestry for five years. He considers himself conservative, strongly patriotic, and highly religious. George's faith has been a source of strength and certainty in the midst of a changing and uncertain world. His congregation has long been an important part of his family's life, providing a positive source of social and moral stability for his children, especially during their adolescence. Worship, vibrant liturgy, prayerful piety, and moral stability constitute what religion means for George Bremer.

For George, religious faith affects persons, not social institutions or systems; it is personal, not social. Honesty, truthfulness, dependability, hard work, respect for the dignity of others—these are the values of his Christian faith at work. Competition and free enterprise in a market economy reward people who work hardest and succeed best in meeting the needs of others. George sees his personal success in the marketplace, along with its financial rewards, as a means to exercise Christian stewardship in business. For George, successful participation in a competitive economy is perfectly consistent with his understanding of the Christian faith.

Over time, George has developed disdain for government programs and mechanisms that intervene in efficient markets to attain other social ends, such as the redistribution of wealth and income or the redistribution of jobs in favor of disadvantaged groups. He believes that markets succeed where governments fail. If only we would leave markets alone, we'd all be better off, including poor people. He thinks most government programs are unethical for their tendency to keep people out of the market economy—thus hurting those they intend to help.

George feels no guilt about his financial wealth. He has earned it fairly and honestly by meeting the economic needs of others more efficiently than his competitors. Resentful of what he perceives as high taxes, he would rather be free to spend his wealth as he chooses, on himself and his family, or through freely chosen charitable causes like his church.

Though George's belief in free markets and competition and his disdain for government intervention seem to have been vindicated by the recent collapse of Soviet-dominated socialism, they have been challenged by other recent global trends. With the continuing exodus of U.S. production facilities to countries with lower-cost labor, George has begun to doubt his strong belief in the benefits of unrestrained labor markets and global competition. He fears that he too runs the risk of becoming economically obsolete and easily replaced by a manager elsewhere in the world for one-fourth his cost. Further, heightened public discussions of environmental problems, such as global warming, the depletion of the ozone layer, and exploding global population growth, make George wonder whether relatively unrestrained market economies will continue to generate such overwhelming social benefit without great social harm. George wonders whether some of the doomsday environmentalists aren't at least partially correct—that the modern era of industrialization and technological advancement may be moving toward a disastrous end, including depletion of energy sources and an increasingly dangerous inheritance of various forms of pollution. George is beginning to feel ill-equipped as a Christian to know how to respond to these new global economic challenges.

JANE COREY

Jane Corey is an energetic forty-two-year-old parish pastor in a liberal Protestant denomination. Previously married with two children, she had been a full-time mother and housewife until her early thirties when she completed college. Feeling a call to ordained ministry, she then attended an ecumenically minded denominational seminary. There, she was exposed to many theological perspectives, including feminist and liberation thought. For Jane, this midlife educational process was transformative in many ways. It broadened and radicalized her perspective so that she saw and critiqued her personal life in new ways and viewed the world, especially its systems, institutions, and social practices, in a new critical light. During this time, her children graduated from high school, and her marriage fell apart as her husband could not accept her new sense of self and vocational identity. She received a call to a congregation in a large eastern city in a diverse urban, multicultural neighborhood adjacent to a large university.

Jane understands the gospel as a power for change in the world, not only for individuals but also for social systems and structures. Consistent with her reading of Scripture, Jane would consider herself a harsh social critic. Her feminist commitments lead her to see the world as a systemic pattern of patriarchal relationships in which men use social power to perpetuate their position of privilege to the continued detriment and exclusion of women. Her liberationist commitments lead her to view society as a coherent pattern of domination in which persons with political and economic power create and maintain social institutions in ways that preserve the privileges of wealth for some to the exclusion of people who are poor, domestically and internationally. Her socialist ideals lead her to believe that capitalist institutions and practices, for the most part, are morally evil. Embodiments of social sin, they encourage the vices of greed, acquisitiveness, and undue concern for the self—all antithetical to gospel values of care, service to neighbor, and concern for communal good. Capitalism, she would also say, is the cause of the growing inequalities of wealth and income that have generated today's severe levels of poverty and marginalization. Jane is more certain about how socialism provides a criticism of the existing capitalist system than for how it might create a constructive institutional alternative. Although she would reject Soviet-style, totalitarian, collectivist models of society, she would advocate a much stronger role for government as a means to control and counterbalance the pervasive power of private wealth and capital in our country and throughout the world.

Jane has strong convictions about the demands of social justice, but she is not a rigid, narrow-minded person. She thrives in an academic setting in which issues are debated openly from a variety of perspectives. Within her congregation, though, she is uncertain how best to express her views and engage her people in debate about the relationship of faith and life in society, especially economic life. A social justice activist herself, she hopes to instill within her members a vision of the congregation as a community of moral deliberation and of social action, where members can commit themselves to transformative, liberating actions and causes. She has taken a first hopeful step by getting a handful of dedicated women from her congregation to join her as volunteers at a local battered women's shelter.

With her antibusiness bias, Jane is unsure how to raise issues of faith and economic life with her many members working within business and the professions, some at middle- and senior-management levels. Would successful ministry mean that these individuals would be convinced to leave their corporate jobs and devote themselves to more community-minded pursuits? Or would success mean that these individuals would remain within their positions of power, working for transformation of business from within? Jane doesn't know what the latter option would look like. At the heart of things, she is fundamentally suspicious that Christians can put faith to work in a capitalist system at all. For Jane, the prophetic and the pastoral dimensions of her congregational ministry seem radically at odds with each other.

MARK O'GRADY

Father Mark O'Grady is a fifty-seven-year-old parish priest at St. Mary's Church. As pastor of a large congregation in a midsized community, Mark ministers to people in diverse economic and professional situations.

Steeped in the tradition of Roman Catholic social teaching, Mark has always had high moral and social expectations of business and economic systems. He believes business managers have strong moral responsibilities to use their power, wealth, and knowledge in ways that benefit society, especially less-advantaged persons. Likewise, he has always believed that government should intervene in business and economic affairs for the sake of the common good, especially on behalf of poor and marginalized persons. Viewing himself as neither a capitalist nor a socialist, he sees Christian ethics and values as pointing toward a more humane third way between these two systems; he believes both have moral faults and problems, at least in their most extreme forms.

Mark often feels torn about how to minister most effectively to his congregation. With managerial, professional, and blue-collar members in the pew, many from the same large corporations, he regularly feels constrained in how far he can go in attempting to clarify the specifics of a prophetic ministry. When a large corporation closed a local production facility, putting dozens of his blue-collar members out of work, he shared their pain and disbelief, and he understood their feelings of resentment and anger against the "profit-hungry" senior managers. At the same time, he tried to listen objectively to his managerial members who claim that such events, though tragic and painful, are inevitable and, in the long run, beneficial for the long-term competitive future of our country's economy. U.S. companies, they argue, have no alternative but constantly to adapt their cost structures and production processes to ever-increasing global economic pressures. In some cases, such as with the facility in his town, that means shutting down an inefficient plant whose high production costs are claimed to be hopelessly beyond the scope of cost-effectiveness.

Mark affirms the grand moral vision espoused by John Paul II in his recent encyclical *Centesimus Annus*. The pope argues that the recent collapse of totalitarian socialism now places an unequivocal moral challenge in the hands of global capitalism to generate humane economic and wholistic human development for all people around the globe, especially poor people in less-developed countries. But Mark feels confused by painful local economic events and conflicting economic explanations of these events. As a Catholic priest and moral teacher informed by the teachings of his church, he is unsure how to understand these events in light of his faith, and he is unsure how to pastor to his people. His seminary training thirty years ago leaves him feeling ill-equipped fully to understand today's complex, global economic realities. He is somewhat unsure how to put his faith to work in exercising pastoral leadership and guidance and how his people should put their faith to work in these changing times.

BYRON NEWCOMB

Byron Newcomb is the forty-eight-year-old president of Newcomb & Associates, a midsized, family-owned advertising agency in a large midwestern city. Byron is a lifelong Roman Catholic who is deeply involved in his local congregation. He attended college at a large, prestigious Roman Catholic university and even considered becoming a missionary priest. He changed his mind, though, and is married with three children. After college, he joined his father's fledgling ad agency, eventually became president, and bought the business when he and his father disagreed about the directions for the business several years ago. Under Byron's leadership, the business has grown steadily.

Throughout his career, he has sought to integrate his faith with his work and his business. Byron has been inspired by Roman Catholic social teaching and by twentieth-century spiritual writers such as Thomas Merton and Albert Schweitzer. Not only is Byron an avid reader of theology and spirituality, but he begins each day with prayer, scripture reading, and quiet meditation. Without being overtly religious, he attempts to create a corporate environment in which his spiritual and ethical values can be freely expressed and embodied in the culture and work of his agency. Respect for all individuals, including clients and employees, an emphasis on teamwork and collaboration, a relative lack of hierarchy and structure within his company, and a deep concern that the company's work reflects positive social values are consistent with Byron's religiously informed vision of a creative, humane, community-nurturing society.

Never a harsh social critic, Byron is by nature optimistic, entrepreneurial, and visionary. He is forever imagining opportunities for individuals to energize systems, institutions, and social practices with positive, transformative social values. Byron would resist the label, but some people would characterize him as a crusader who seeks to transform the world from within prevailing social institutions. A firm believer in capitalism and the market, he has confident hope in the capacity of religious values to inspire and transform the practices of consumers, workers, entrepreneurs, managers, and private sector institutions in a democratic capitalist society. For Byron, work is a sacrament, a means for God to breathe vitality into human society. He is a Christian first and a capitalist second, but he strives to merge the two in a creative, and in his mind usually successful, tension.

Byron has no illusions about the difficulty of applying faith and spirituality to his business. He sees this integration as a creative, intuitive, sometimes uncertain, and ambiguous challenge. Byron struggles with the dilemma of what to do with underperforming employees; his desire to make extra efforts to nurture and inspire better performance from them is offset by his awareness of the severe competitive pressures on his business that force him to demand excellent work from all employees. A person who believes in loyalty to company and loyalty to employees, he strives to avoid layoffs due to fluctuations in business cycles, even when he will personally have to sacrifice profits.

As an advertiser, Byron is concerned that the products he is asked to advertise have positive social value and that they be advertised in morally appropriate ways. He refuses to advertise certain products that he considers morally harmful to society, including tobacco and alcoholic beverages. When asked to advertise a military toy in a way that would portray violence and loss of human life, Byron resisted and instead convinced his client to advertise the toy in a way that demonstrated its potential life-saving uses.

To the dismay of some of his managers and employees, he has declined some business because he believes that the products do not embody and encourage social values consistent with his religious commitments and vision of the world. They would argue that Byron's religion and ethics sometimes get in the way of his ability to run the business effectively. On a regular basis, though, Byron wrestles with knowing whether his decisions are the right ones. He wonders if his commitments and actions really make a difference in the world. In private moments, away from colleagues and clients, he admits that his profession is morally ambiguous and wonders whether his business demands sometimes force him to compromise his Christian faith and values more than he would like to acknowledge.

BARB DANIELS

Barb Daniels is a thirty-six-year-old African American who works as a sales representative for a large U.S. steel manufacturer in a large urban metropolitan area. A first-generation college graduate, Barb worked her way through night school for six years and, at age twenty-four, was hired as a customer sales representative for a steel company. Two years later, she joined her present company in a comparable position. In an industry that was historically white male oriented, Barb was among the first waves of women and minorities who were hired to respond to new government equal employment opportunity guidelines and to growing pressures by local community activist groups to make more jobs available to persons of color.

Barb is an active member of Ebenezer Baptist Church. This African American congregation has been the mainstay of her life since she was a child. Vibrant preaching, energetic gospel music, and passionate lay involvement in worship have made Sunday morning worship the center of her week and a constant source of spiritual and personal renewal. Her church community is a haven and refuge from a white world that she regularly experiences as hostile and unfair to persons of color such as herself. Barb finds strength and comfort through her faith in a loving God who hears the cry of oppressed people and who offers care and compassion for persons suffering unjustly. She feels nurtured by her fellow members who share her daily experience of racism and exclusion. She feels empowered by her trust in a God who declares injustice, poverty, and racism wrong. Her faith teaches her to believe that she is called to denounce these injustices as evil and to work where she can to make the world a better place. Jesus, her personal savior, is also Christ, her liberator, who offers the full promise of the kingdom of God.

Barb's faith helps her to explain and to cope with discrimination at work. For ten years, Barb has seen many women and African Americans join her company at entry-level professional positions, only to leave within a few years, citing discomfort with the prevailing white male corporate culture. Her rate of promotion has seemed inordinately slow. Barb has seen herself passed over for promotions many times in favor of white males she perceives as no more highly qualified than she. Seven years ago, Barb struggled with a supervisor who would not permit her to interact with certain principal customers in her role as customer service representative because the supervisor claimed the customers were not ready to relate to a black female. Four years ago, Barb filed an internal sexual harassment grievance against a former supervisor. After an anxiety-producing investigation, Barb won her case, and the supervisor was dismissed. During that period, Barb seriously considered leaving the company, not knowing whether she had the courage to endure the pain of being a whistle-blower and the risk of ruining her career within the company.

Barb has been successful at her job and has received promotions, but work is a daily struggle for self-respect, and dignity. Although her organization's most blatant patterns and practices of racism and sexism have disappeared, she still feels herself confronted with a white male management structure that has yet to understand how it uses its privileges and power in ways that often favor white men and disfavor women and persons of color. Her faith provides her with the courage to endure at work. Her faith also provides her with a liberating vision of social values that tells her that aspects of her work and her organization are wrong and unjust, and do not embody the ideals of a just and redeemed world. Barb is not so clear about how her faith might help her to move strategically from her current reality of struggle and discrimination toward the ideals of the Kingdom—whether and how her faith might enable her to transform her current socially sinful work reality into one that better approximates her religious vision of the world. The challenge seems daunting, the thought itself exhausting, as she tries to be a highly competent employee at work while juggling family and parenting responsibilities at home.

These five vignettes characterize some ways that Christians, both clergy and laity, try to connect faith and work. They by no means fully capture the rich diversity of religious traditions, occupations, geography, and personal experiences that combine to make our lives unique. They do represent some typical connections that many Americans make as they envision and live out their Christian ethics at work. Perhaps you can see some of their experiences and perspectives within yourself or other persons you know. Perhaps they can be reference points as you clarify and deepen your Christian ethic at work. Throughout the book, we will refer to these persons to show how they might wrestle with various workplace issues and challenges.

QUESTIONS FOR GROUP STUDY AND DISCUSSION

1. How do you personally relate your faith to your work?

2. In what ways do you struggle with or are you unsure about how to relate your faith to your work?

3. What are the most critical ethical issues and concerns that you face in the workplace and in economic life?

4. In what ways do the religious life and the practice of your congregation address the spiritual and ethical concerns and challenges of work and economic life? How do they fail?

---

5. Within your congregation, do members ever discuss work and economic issues in light of faith? If not, why not?

6. What needs and aspirations would you like to have met within your religious life and within your congregation in terms of relating your faith to your work?

CHAPTER TWO

The World of Work

How Things Look from Within

IF WE ARE TO UNDERSTAND fully the work lives of persons such as George Bremer, Byron Newcomb, and Barb Daniels, as well as our own, we must step back and look at the world of work in its broadest scope. We need to shift for a moment from the personal and move to the level of systems, institutions, and general economic trends. Such matters may seem highly complex and impersonal because they are! But they are ultimately very real and personal. These larger economic forces and trends inevitably shape our work lives and the organizations where we work. The realities that we discuss in this chapter are inherently difficult to grasp, for me and for most readers. I encourage you to hang in there and tackle these complicated issues with me. Understanding them will also shed light on our moral challenges and dilemmas and will influence how we interpret and respond to them.

Economic systems and business organizations provide structure and content for our lives. Shaped by human history, these systems and institutions stand larger than any of us. They bear down on us, with good and ill effects. They shape our choices and our work relationships. They affect both our vision of life's possibilities and our understanding of life's constraints. They are a part of the givenness of life where we must struggle to determine what it means to be a Christian in the world.

As we move into the twenty-first century, we must attempt a fresh description of the world of work, for that world is changing at a revolutionary pace. Recent global events and current trends may make the issues that define the twenty-first century very different from those that have defined the twentieth century. An adequate Christian ethic at work must come to terms with that new, emergent reality. To this task, then, we must turn, as we attempt to sketch some of these changes in the world of work in its global, organizational and managerial dimensions.

THE NEW CONTEXT FOR WORK: THE GLOBAL MARKET ECONOMY

This new economy in which we work is the global market economy. Let me highlight some of its most distinctive features.

Global Integration. A global economy means that our economic transactions move outward across national borders to form an ever larger web of interconnectedness throughout the world. Of course, this reality did not spring up overnight. International trade existed in the Roman Empire; medieval Europe established trading routes with the Far East; the North American colonies were linked economically to their European nation-state parents, as the Latin American colonies were to Spain and Portugal. Multinational corporations have generated significant transnational trade and foreign direct investment for over a century. The transition to a global economy is centuries old, but the process has now developed such momentum that it constitutes a major shift in perspective.

Numerous international developments show that economic life is global to a degree unprecedented in history, a trend that will make the global economy a fact of life in the twenty-first century. We can cite the following as evidence:

- the explosive growth in international trade, increasing more than fourfold in constant U.S. dollars from 1960 to a 1987 level of more than $3 trillion; since the mid-1950s, growth in world trade has significantly exceeded the growth in world GDP (gross domestic product),
- the explosive global growth of foreign direct investment, increasing sevenfold from 1967 ($105 billion) to 1987 ($776 billion),
- the emergence of Japan as a formidable, mature global economic actor and the dramatic growth of other Asian economies on the Pacific Rim,
- the growth of Western European economies, typified by the European Union's drive to create a single unified European economic market, with prospects to integrate Eastern European economies into the fold as well,
- the trend toward continued reductions in trade barriers through multilateral (e.g., General Agreement on Tariffs and Trade), regional (e.g., North American Free Trade Agreement), and bilateral agreements,
- the integration of national capital markets into a single global capital market, characterized by larger computerized flows of funds between countries and more equalized costs of capital among countries,
- most poignantly, perhaps, the collapse of socialism in Eastern Europe and in the former Soviet Union, with the transformation of these economies into market economies, eventually competitive in the global economy,
- a growing cultural homogeneity among developed countries, as seen by the growing availability of popular brand-name products around the globe.

This inexorable drive toward global economic integration is well illustrated by Robert Reich's description of what it means to have purchased a recent GM Pontiac Le Mans:

> Of the $10,000 paid to GM, about $3,000 goes to South Korea for routine labor and assembly operations, $1,750 to Japan for advanced components (engines, transaxles, and electronics), $750 to Germany for styling and design engineering, $400 to Taiwan, Singapore, and Japan for small components, $250 to Britain for advertising and marketing services, and about $50 to Ireland and Barbados for data processing. The rest—less than $4,000—goes to strategists in Detroit, lawyers and bankers in New York, lobbyists in Washington, insurance, and health-care workers all over the country, and General Motors shareholders—most of whom live in the United States, but an increasing number of whom are foreign nationals. (*The Work of Nations*, 113)

Increased Competitiveness. As domestic economies and corporations move beyond their borders with trade, production, investment, and marketing, they build a web of economic interdependence that becomes increasingly inextricable. With the relentless drive to erode economic barriers to freer trade and markets, competitive advantage will continue to be the primary determinant for economic survival and development. As markets for capital, land, labor, and consumer goods become increasingly international, moving freely across political borders, competition will intensify. In this process a downward cost spiral will push firms to enhance productivity and quality while containing production costs. Traditionally high-cost producers in mature industries from countries like the United States, Germany, and now even Japan will continue to feel pressure from new international competitors who force them to lower prices and/or increase quality to survive.

Technological Change. Rapid changes in production and communications technologies will also continue to revolutionize work across the globe.

> The incredible changes in the core technologies facing the global economy—microelectronics, biotechnology, and advanced materials—have virtually no precedent in world history. Each on its own will make obsolete all that precedes it. Each will bring revolutionary implications as well as applications across a host of products and services. (McMillan and Wright, "Services," 104)

New process technologies, for which the Japanese have become so proficient, continue to drive down the costs of many consumer products. Americans create new products; the Japanese learn to produce them more cheaply and often at higher quality. Electronics and new materials result in lighter, more compact products less costly to ship. Transportation costs are falling. Increased ease of communication and data transfer help to link operations in different countries. Aided by information technology, firms integrate and coordinate far-flung activities in more complex ways in manufacturing, logistics, research and development, and other areas. Information flows more freely between buyers and sellers. In sum, rapid technological change increases the importance and speed of innovation and also reduces the extent to which geography is a barrier to economic activity, thereby reinforcing the drive toward economic globalization.

Shift from Manufacturing to Services. Since World War II, Western economies have shifted from industrial manufacturing toward services. Some see this trend ominously as a process of deindustrialization for countries like the United States; others see a more benign trend. For instance, U.S. manufacturing employment rose from 15.2 million workers in 1950 to 20.3 million in 1980. Within U.S. manufacturing from 1973 to 1979, industries with rapid rates of technological innovation increased their employment share by 9 percent, while industries with mature technology decreased their employment by 6 percent. The *percentage* share of manufacturing output has declined in the past three decades, but the *volume* of output has grown steadily. The actual situation may be not deindustrialization but rapid and steady economic growth in service sectors (e.g., finance, retailing, advertising, leasing, transportation, communications). As the world's industrial economies move toward global economic integration, services, broadly defined, will account for some two-thirds of our gross domestic product. Some claim that the growth of a massive infrastructure of companies and industries to support the global manufacturing sector will make real distinctions between manufacturing and services increasingly irrelevant. Some describe this global shift as the emergence of the new information economy.

Global Corporations. International business, which involves the crossing of national borders, is not new, nor are multinational corporations. According to the United Nations Centre on Transnational Corporations, the six hundred largest multinational corporations account for between one-fifth and one-fourth of the value added in the production of all goods in the world's market economies. The emergence of the global corporation, though, is a relatively new phenomenon. Some persons characterized the earlier twentieth-century multinational corporation as a type of holding company with a number of overseas operations, each of which adapted its products and marketing strategy to what local managers thought were the unique aspects of their individual markets. The rationale for foreign operations often was quite modest—to generate a safety-valve market for excess production in domestic markets. The global firm is characterized as "a firm that attempts to standardize op-

THE WORLD OF WORK

erations in all functional areas, but that responds to national market differences when necessary" (Ball and McCullough, *International Business,* p. 18) and "a series of linked domestic industries in which the rivals compete against each other on a truly worldwide basis" (Porter, *Competition in Global Industries,* p. 18). The global corporation exploits production and communications technology in the effort to become a highly integrated, coordinated productive organism.

Michael Porter writes:

> If the old agenda for international firms was how to deal with foreign market circumstances, then the pressing new agenda is both broader and different. It is how to manage established networks of far-flung overseas activities as a single, effective unit. Firms are searching for ways to convert worldwide production, marketing, research and development, and financial presence into a competitive advantage. They face both pressures and offers of support from home and host governments and must decide when and how to respond. Firms are confronting also a bewildering array of coalitions among international competitors, as well as pressing management problems of implementing their own inter-firm agreements. Finally, they struggle continually, against vexing organizational barriers, to coordinate units located around the globe to work together. Global competition is no longer a trend but a reality. (*Competition in Global Industries,* 11)

All these trends—global integration, increased competitiveness, rapid and revolutionary technological change, the shift from manufacturing to services, and the growth of global corporations—were in place before the collapse of socialism. Yet socialism's collapse seems to solidify their impact and speed up their reach into geographic regions once off-limits. There will no longer be two more or less segregated industrialized economic systems, each with its own territorial influence—one capitalist, one centrally planned. Rather, there will be only one game in town—an integrated global market economy. The question will no longer be which game to play but who will play and by what rules. Though capitalism is becoming a unifying global reality, it will continue to show its many varieties of local color. U.S. capitalism will continue to differ significantly from Japanese and European forms of capitalism.

If the twentieth century was defined primarily by the cosmic battle between pluralism and communism, the twenty-first century will likely be defined by the challenge to structure the global economy in ways that seek economic development of *all* nations as well as environmental protection. Who plays the game in the twenty-first century will depend much on how we structure the rules of the game.

As the world's economy steps out of its capitalist versus socialist straitjacket, it is reshaping itself into three regional economic spheres of influence and interdependence— North America, Europe, and Japan. At the same time, there is uncertainty about the future economic prospects of the rest of the world, most notably less-developed economies of the Southern Hemisphere. The economic rules of the game are being restructured on all fronts—regionally and multi-laterally. Their outcomes will be critical to the future economic prospects of all economies, rich and poor alike.

Within the Western Hemisphere, the North American Free Trade Agreement (NAFTA) will link the economies of Canada, the United States, and Mexico in ways that will rapidly expand trade and affect patterns of investment and production among them—all presumably to the benefit of consumers from all three nations, resulting in stronger economic growth for the region. Within Western Europe, the European Union (EU) continues to push toward full economic integration, with future efforts that will likely widen its geographic circle of interdependence to include formerly socialist countries and even create greater political integration. Barriers to trade will surely fall *within* these regions. The question remains whether higher trade barriers will be created with those *outside* each region. For example, will the European Union continue to restrict goods such as agricultural products from Eastern European countries, which desire fuller access to EU markets? Will NAFTA place products from Latin America at a competitive disadvantage to those from Mexico in U.S. markets, thus constraining Latin America's economic development?

Within less-developed countries, many governments have consented to painful adjustments requiring radical changes in monetary and fiscal policies. These changes aim to reduce government spending and deficits, control rates of inflation, and stimulate the growth of private sector employment by encouraging liberal trade, more active competition, and open markets. Coupled with this trend is the new General Agreement on Tariffs and Trade (GATT), the overarching multilateral trade treaty that provides the basic rules governing global trade. Will GATT, which aims in principle to liberalize global trade, contribute to stronger economic growth and prosperity for less-developed nations, or will it result in exclusion and economic stagnation? The future prospects of the less-developed world hang in the balance in this new global market economy, as do the uncertain economic prospects of the republics of the former Soviet Union.

This broad portrayal of the global market economy may seem extremely abstract and far removed from day-to-day realities in our worlds of work. Nevertheless, these trends are very real, for they affect us all and will do so even more dramatically in the future. George Bremer faces them daily as he determines where to locate his plants, what new technologies should drive his production facilities, and how he can retain and retrain as many of his workers as possible in the midst of such radical changes. Barb Daniels is daily reminded of these transformations as she sees her steel company competing with low-cost foreign producers and as her sales team identifies more foreign customers. And as a parish pastor, Mark O'Grady often feels more and more challenged to understand the increasingly complex global economy.

Most U.S. workers employed in the manufacturing sector and in some other sectors have been affected by increased global integration and competition. The U.S. auto industry is a prime example. As many U.S. consumers have shifted their purchases to higher quality cars made by Japanese companies, U.S. auto manufacturers have declined in U.S. market share. U.S. auto manufacturers have reduced their workforces by more than two hundred thousand over the past fifteen years and are likely to continue the reduction throughout the 1990s. Dislocation and at least temporary trauma and economic hardship for many more will occur. Labor costs for U.S. autoworkers have been reduced as domestic labor markets have been forced to compete in a broader, lower-priced global market. U.S. auto companies have become more quality and cost conscious. Hundreds of thousands of American autoworkers are now employed by foreign auto manufacturers, most notably Japanese. In 1991, for example, ten thousand U.S. workers at Honda's facility in Marysville, Ohio, assembled the most popular car sold in the United States—the Honda Accord. The U.S. auto industry's experience has been mirrored in industry after industry, such as consumer electronics, computers, semiconductors, and retailing. Where we work, how we work, what we produce, what we're paid, what we buy, how we allocate capital—all these factors have been affected by the evolution and growth of the global market economy.

THE EVOLVING NATURE OF OUR WORK ORGANIZATIONS

Most of us who work are employed by others and work in organizations. Only 6 percent are self-employed. In 1994, 75 percent of U.S. workers were employed in the private and nonprofit sectors, 16 percent were in federal, state, or local government, and 3 percent were in agriculture. Our choices and decisions at work are shaped and constrained by bosses, coworkers, and subordinates. Few, if any of us, have complete discretion and freedom in what we do at work. Rather, we act within a web of relationships and responsibilities. Our actions are influenced by organizational objectives, organizational cultures, job descriptions, directives from bosses, relations and shared responsibilities with coworkers, and responsibilities of people who report to us. Work is inherently social and, for most of us, increasingly complex.

Describing contemporary work organizations is nearly as illusive and impossible as making generalizations about the global economy. The rich diversity of organizations defies easy description and analysis. Work organizations vary in purpose, type of ownership, size, structure, and style in ways that we cannot come close to fully capturing here. They can be examined and analyzed by numerous disciplines and fields of vision (e.g., sociology, industrial psychology, economics, organization behavior, management theories) that lie beyond the scope of this book.

Increased global competition and integration and rapid technological innovation are radically and continuously changing the structure of modern work organizations. This process has been most pronounced in the private sector. In the United States, increased competition and globalization have placed fierce and relentless pressure on businesses to reduce their costs of production, most significantly in labor. As a result, for at least the past decade, U.S. firms have responded with wave upon wave of workforce reductions, among semiskilled and routine production workers as well as at managerial and professional levels. No level of worker has been exempt from threat of job loss, from CEO (when boards of directors fire CEOs or when companies merge) to middle managers to shop floor workers. In "the good old days" before global competition, some U.S. firms, especially those insulated within highly regulated industries such as telecommunications, could provide virtual guarantees of lifetime employment. Those days now seem gone forever. Increased competition and technological innovation bring lower costs and enhanced productivity—benefits to consumers; however, their inevitable handmaidens are diminished job security and longevity and increased employment mobility. We can expect the pace of worker obsolescence to increase in the next century, raising questions of social responsibility for governments, corporations, and workers themselves, an issue to which we will return in chapter 5.

Technological innovations will change work organizations in countless ways, many of which we cannot anticipate with certainty. Computerized data processing began to make its mark in the 1950s; its technological advances will make possible new business configurations that will make predecessors obsolete. For example, future technological breakthroughs in microelectronics and microcomputing could make possible entirely new ways to make telephone calls, forcing a radical transformation of the telecommunications industry and the way it relates to other industries and technologies such as entertainment and television. The U.S. government-initiated process that began in 1984 mandating the breakup of the AT&T telecommunications monopoly into a series of semiregulated regional telephone companies may come to its final deregulated culmination. Process technology innovation, for which the Japanese have become so expert, will change the ways that people and materials are combined in ever more efficient ways to produce higher quality goods.

Some have defined the process by which technology is transforming organizations and work as *reengineering*. This term embraces such techniques as using work teams; training employees in multiple skills so that they can do more than one job; empowering employees, which means pushing decision-making authority as far down in an organization as possible; and reorganizing assembly lines and offices to simplify and speed the work flow. Our aim is to restructure work in response to continual technological innovations in ways that improve worker productivity. George Bremer struggles to keep abreast of this process on a regular basis. Some estimate that this process eventually may eliminate as many as 25 million more jobs from the U.S. private sector, which currently encompasses roughly 90 million jobs!

Clearly, global corporations will play a prominent role in the global market economy. Global business is and will become an even larger fact of life. Technological advances in communication and transportation, lowered trade barriers, convergences of consumer tastes around the world, and decreased costs of capital in a more freely flowing global capital market combine to lower the costs and increase the opportunities of global business. What kinds of companies will be most effective and successful in this business environment? Will multibillion-dollar firms employing hundreds of thousands of people, such as GM, IBM, Motorola, Philips, and Toyota, be most successful? Will their size permit them to capitalize on economies of scale and huge research and development investments that smaller firms cannot afford? Or will smaller, more nimble firms adapt most effectively to growing global opportunities, constraints, and markets?

What kinds of places will large as well as small corporations be to work? Some predict that global corporations will be highly centralized, hierarchical organizations that attempt to control all phases of product development, production, marketing, and distribution across the globe. Nations will develop highly competitive clusters of firms within related industry groups that develop global "comparative advantage." Robert Reich argues that global corporations will most effectively become decentralized "networks" of loosely configured, ever-changing associations among highly specialized business units that contract together for limited purposes. In such an organization, success will not depend on control of capital, ownership of physical assets, or employment of a large, permanent workforce. These may become cumbersome liabilities that hinder effective, rapid response to consumer demand. Rather, the effective global company will consist essentially of the creative, managerial, and coordinating acumen necessary to bring together all the talents, labor, capital, production facilities, and other business components into loose contractual alliances for limited and discrete periods of time, only to be reconfigured and renegotiated for future projects.

Life within such business organizations would be contractual, highly dynamic, and subject to constant change. High productivity, creativity, the capacity to identify and solve problems, and the willingness and ability to adapt and "retool" will be the qualities that permit workers to survive and thrive. More stress and uncertainty may also be by-products of this organizational trend. Whether organizations get high levels of commitment and productivity from their workers at the same time that job tenure and security are diminishing is an issue to which we will return in chapter 5.

Despite the focus on global corporations, most new job creation in the United States is through smaller entrepreneurial firms, not through large Fortune 500 companies. Some larger trends suggest this may continue in the global economy. New technologies, notably in computers and process technologies, are narrowing the economies of scale in manufacturing and distribution, making it possible to produce goods cheaply in smaller volumes. The falling prices of computers make it easier for smaller firms to use the same logistical techniques, financial models, and automated administrative tasks that were available only to larger firms in the past. The internationalization of capital markets has driven down the cost of capital and has permitted some medium-sized firms to raise money in the same ways very large firms have.

What will it be like to work in organizations struggling to survive by staying abreast of technological innovation and remaining competitive in an increasingly integrated global economy? Life will be even more fast paced than before, a claim that each generation makes in relation to all that has preceded it! Organizations will demand higher levels of productivity from workers. For many of us, these demands will likely make our relationships with our work organizations feel less permanent and more insecure. The demands of high performance bring higher levels of uncertainty and stress for many, facts of life that must be managed if we are to live healthfully. The paradox is that as labor, especially highly skilled labor, as a factor of production becomes more important, organizations may be less able to protect it with assurances of long-term employment. At the same time, highly skilled workers such as managers will be given greater responsibility and decision-making authority as layers of management are eliminated due to competitive pressures to cut production costs.

Furthermore, life at work will differ according to one's place in the organization. Based on occupational trends that we can anticipate continuing into the future, the modern workplace will produce winners and losers in terms of prospects for employment and earnings. Over the past several years, the only U.S. workers whose earnings have kept pace with inflation have been college-educated people. Robert Reich divides workers into three categories: "symbolic analysts" (most managerial and professional functions), in-person service workers, and routine production workers.

Prospects for enhanced employment and earnings are positive only for "symbolic analysts."

Finally, work organizations will continue to grow in their cultural and ethnic diversity. Not only will the growth of global corporations tend to cross-fertilize national and ethnic boundaries through increased overseas assignments, but larger demographic trends will make cultural and ethnic diversity in the U.S. workplace a more pronounced reality. The vast majority of new entrants into the U.S. workforce are foreign born, nonwhite, and/or female. Organizations that wish to survive and thrive in this multicultural climate will learn to open their doors and adapt their policies and practices to make workplace diversity an asset rather than a perceived liability.

In sum, this new world of work is global, highly complex and technologically sophisticated, and rapidly changing. Our work organizations will continue to adapt to these larger systemic changes as they struggle to survive and thrive in a more competitive and changing environment. Likewise, the specific occupational roles that we hold in the workforce will continue to evolve as we are called on to acquire and demonstrate new skills and abilities that effectively respond to marketplace demands and needs. This is the new economic reality in which we find ourselves today and in which we must attempt to discern what it means to be a Christian and how we will go about putting our Christian ethics to work.

QUESTIONS FOR GROUP STUDY AND DISCUSSION

1. How would you characterize today's global economy?

2. How do these economic trends affect your work and the organization for which you work?

3. How would you describe the organization for which you work?

4. How do its organizational structure, culture, and style affect the role you play and the work you do?

5. How do you anticipate that your work organization and your work will change in the next ten to twenty years?

KEY RESOURCES

Ball, Donald, and Wendell H. McCullough, Jr. *International Business: Introduction and Essentials.* 4th ed. Homewood, Ill.: BPI/Irwin, 1990.

Berger, Peter L. *The Capitalist Revolution: Fifty Propositions About Prosperity, Equality, and Liberty.* New York: Basic Books, 1986.

McMillan, Charles J. and Nigel S. Wright. "Services: Changing Perspectives on the Global Economy." *Business in the Contemporary World,* Spring 1991, 102-12.

Moran, Theodore H. *Multinational Corporations: The Political Economy of Foreign Direct Investment.* Lexington, Mass.: Lexington Books, 1985.

Porter, Michael E., ed. *Competition in Global Industries.* Boston: Harvard Business School Press, 1986.

————. *The Competitive Advantage of Nations.* New York: Free Press, 1990.

Reich, Robert. *The Work of Nations: Preparing Ourselves for 21st Century Capitalism.* New York: Knopf, 1991.

Thurow, Lester. *Head to Head: The Coming Economic Battle Among Japan, Europe, and America.* New York: Morrow, 1992.

CHAPTER THREE

Christian Ethics

Claiming the Vision and Language of Faith

NOW THAT WE HAVE looked briefly at today's global economy, we need to ask how our Christian faith can provide vision, values, directives, and guidance for our lives at work. What distinctive concepts can we lift up from Christian faith, Scripture, and theology that can be defining features of a Christian ethic at work? How might we construct a theological ethic for business and economic life? How can we claim the language of faith in a way that offers direction for our lives at work?

First, we need to recognize the rich diversity of perspectives among believers and Christian faith communities. There is no single, monolithic way to relate Christian faith to our work. Even within each faith community, a diversity of ethical approaches can be identified. Each may be legitimately and coherently grounded in different parts of a tradition. Each may emerge from different experiences of believers within the community. There is no escaping this pluralism, and it is therefore worthwhile to look at various theological and ethical themes, values, and ideas that have been important to believers across the centuries. I present some Christian ethical concepts as a basis for your vision and language of faith for your world of work.

Try to interpret them in light of your faith tradition. Try to imagine their creative possibilities for constructing a life of faith in your workplace. All five Christians portrayed in this book have claimed the language of faith and have drawn on at least some of these concepts in different and distinctive ways. Your challenge is to do the same.

DIVINE SOVEREIGNTY

Praise the LORD!
Praise the LORD from the heavens;
   praise him in the heights!
Praise him, all his angels;
   praise him, all his host!

Praise him, sun and moon;
   praise him, all you shining stars!
Praise him, you highest heavens,
   and you waters above the heavens!

Let them praise the name of the LORD,
   for he commanded and they were created.
He established them forever and ever;
   he fixed their bounds, which cannot be passed. . . .

Let them praise the name of the LORD,
   for his name alone is exalted;
   his glory is above earth and heaven.

(Ps. 148:1-6, 13)

God created the world and is sovereign over it. This political image portrays God as powerful ruler who has authority and control over God's subjects, who in turn are asked to be obedient to God. Such an autocratic concept may seem antiquated to our modern, democratic ears. Some theologians argue that other less-authoritarian metaphors (e.g., God as friend, parent, partner) are more appropriate for portraying our understandings of God in the modern world.

But with appropriate qualifications, divine sovereignty can remain a viable theological concept for modern Christians. We believe that God created the world good. And God did not merely create the world and then let it go its own way. Rather, sovereignty implies an *ongoing* relationship between ruler and ruled. Furthermore, Hebrew and Christian scriptures portray sovereignty as beneficial to humans—care, protection, and order are characteristics of this dominion. God, the sovereign, continues to show care for the created world.

Because God created all that exists, nothing exists outside God's sovereign order. All of creation falls under God's sacred canopy. This includes social life and the natural world—politics, economics, family and personal life, and our relationship to nature. Hence, work and economic life fall within God's divine sovereignty and order. There can be no separation of sacred and secular. Far from being irrelevant, what we do within economic life takes on religious significance (even though we are not justified by our works).

To say that God is sovereign over all that exists, including economic life, is to imply that God's purposes can be known not only through Scripture and Christian tradition but also through social and economic realities, institutions, practices, and personal experiences. That is, God can and does work through organizations and institutions of all sorts. The challenging task, then, becomes discerning God's sovereign intentions for work and economic life. What are God's purposes for economic life, and how do we best go about cooperating with them? Is there a moral structure and order that should guide our action and conduct at work? If so, what are they, and how do we discern them? What are the sources for knowing God's intentions for the world? They can include Scripture, reason, human sciences, and human experience. These are classic questions within the Christian faith. We must continue to struggle with them.

WORK AS THE STEWARDSHIP OF CREATION

> God blessed them [male and female], and God said to them, "Be fruitful and multiply, and fill the earth and subdue it; and have dominion over the fish of the sea and over the birds of the air and over every living thing that moves upon the earth." (Gen. 1:28)

These words from the creation account tell us many things. God created the world. The world was created good, not flawed. Humans are blessed by God and have special place and perhaps even priority in creation. We are given a mandate for work and economic life. In its broadest sense, work has religious value and meaning. Its purpose, defined by God, is to sustain our lives and to be stewards of creation. Work involves our interaction with nature, using and transforming its living and nonliving aspects, at least in part, for our benefit. Work becames a way that we are called to care for creation.

On the surface, these words seem to convey that humans have primary value in creation. Furthermore, hierarchical concepts like dominion have been thought by some to justify domination over nature, devaluation of nature, and even abuse of nature for short-term human gain. Only recently have Christian ethicists begun to look more carefully and critically at the ways in which Scripture and theology have shaped our ethical orientation toward nature and the environment. For the most part, nature either has been ignored as a topic of moral consideration or has been viewed as having only instrumental value—as existing *only* for the sake of human well-being, permitting its degradation and abuse as a result of human activity. Some religious scholars would argue that the very concepts of stewardship and dominion must be discarded, given their tendencies to place humans above nature in ways that have been severely destructive to ecological sustainability and, ultimately, to human sustainability on the planet. We will return to this topic in greater depth in chapter 5.

For our purposes, we can say that the creation account in Genesis provides positive moral support for the human activity of work itself. In this sense, we believe that work is a part of our religious nature as persons created by God. Furthermore, humans are authorized by God through our work to use the goods of nature for our benefit.

At the same time, we cannot ignore Genesis's second word about work—that work is a curse. For Genesis 3 tells us that God makes work difficult and sometimes painful, even as punishment for our rebellion against God: "In toil you shall eat of it all the days of your life. . . . By the sweat of your face you shall eat bread" (Gen. 3:17, 19). Although work is created good and intended for us by God, our experience of it can be difficult and toilsome. We ought not to expect that our efforts will always yield easy, beneficial results. Work can also be frustrating, painful, and sometimes fruitless. Christians must acknowledge our work as tainted by sin, yet our larger affirmation is its fundamental goodness.

Within a work organization, how can Christians as workers embody the mandate to be stewards of creation? How can we understand business managers as stewards? Managers with varying levels of power and authority are entrusted with the coordination and oversight of resources within an organization—people, capital, production processes, technology. Our faith encourages us to see these responsibilities as a part of our religious identity and as a way to live out a religious vision of faith.

WORK AS VOCATION

Each one should do the works of his profession and station, not that by them he may strive after righteousness, but that through them he may keep his body under control, be an example to others who also need to keep their bodies

under control, and finally that by such works he may submit
his will to that of others in the freedom of love.

(Luther, "The Freedom of a Christian")

Related to the theme of stewardship is the concept of
vocation. Martin Luther gives us its classic formulation.
Though all Christians are justified by faith alone and not by
works, the work of Christians in the world is nevertheless vital
to our life of faith. Freed from relying on our inadequate and
sinful actions to win God's acceptance, we are called to a life
of grateful response to God's gracious acceptance of us
through our faith in Jesus Christ. Our calling as Christians,
our vocation in the world, is to devote ourselves to serving
the good of the neighbor and the community in every sphere
of life, including family and personal relationships, our role
as citizens, and our work.

Gone is the rigid dividing line between sacred and secular
and between priest and layperson. As the clergyperson is
called to do God's work in the world, so are all other Christians called to fulfill God's intentions in our work, whatever
the occupation happens to be. Our secular occupations are
sacred and become the religious arenas within which we are
called to fulfill our vocation, our calling, as Christians in the
world—to serve the good of the neighbor and the community.

In their 1986 pastoral letter, *Economic Justice for All,* the
U.S. Roman Catholic bishops cite teachings of Pope John
Paul II that see a threefold moral significance in work:

First, it is a principal way that people exercise the distinctive human capacity for self-expression and self-realization.
Second, it is the ordinary way for human beings to fulfill their
material needs. Finally, work enables people to contribute to
the well-being of the larger community. Work is not only for
one's self. It is for one's family, for the nation, and indeed
for the benefit of the entire human family. (#97)

To claim that we are called to seek a vocation of service to neighbor and community within our various occupations is an idealistic and demanding concept. What does it mean to serve the good of the neighbor and the community in the roles that we fulfill at work? How do we know when we are doing this well? Does every kind of work lend itself equally well to vocational service to the neighbor? Byron Newcomb tries to serve the community by creating advertising that has positive social value and does not encourage harm to society or to the consumer. George Bremer tries to serve society by keeping his company competitive, thus providing meaningful employment and high-quality products. And surely, Jane Corey hopes that her members will be inspired and made courageous by faith to seek the good of society within their work roles.

Many organizations are so large and bureaucratic and their functions so complex that employees do not regularly see the results of their labor. When the service or contribution of each individual is merely one of hundreds or thousands that combine to form the end product or service, feeling a full sense of vocational satisfaction can sometimes be extremely difficult. Many of us never see the customer, client, or end user. Often, we feel as if we know neither the neighbor nor his or her good whose purpose the job is to serve.

What if we have moral objections to the goods or services that our organization produces or the ways in which the organization does its business? What if we believe the structure of the organization impedes our job performance and fulfillment of vocation? As Christians, when must we accept the imperfect people, conditions, and structures of work life around us and yet persevere in serving the neighbor as best we can in our work? And when, on the other hand, should we try to challenge and transform the people and structures of work life that bear down on us because our faith and ethics compel us to do so? These questions are nearly impossible to answer in the abstract. Our discussions of human dignity and justice may point us in the right direction. We will return to these questions again in later chapters.

SIN

So when the woman saw that the tree was good for food, and that it was a delight to the eyes, and that the tree was to be desired to make one wise, she took of its fruit and ate; and she also gave some to her husband, who was with her, and he ate. (Gen. 3:6)

Surely Christians must bring with us an understanding of sin into our workplaces. Throughout Christian history, sin has developed many meanings and applications. They include sin as idolatry, disbelief, selfishness, sloth, misuse of power, injustice, the breakdown of moral community, the violation of human rights, and the abuse of nature. Our theological traditions have also developed many responses to sin and strategies for how to confront it, including pacifism, just war, perfectionist aversion, and loving transformation. What is sin? To what extent must we acknowledge it as a permanent reality of the human condition? To what extent can we confront, minimize, and transform it? What does it mean to be both justified and sanctified and yet still sinner? Does sin reside in the human heart and/or in structures of society? We must face these questions as we try to keep faith at work.

Genesis portrays humanity's first sin as idolatry. By eating fruit from the tree of knowledge of good and evil, forbidden to them by God, Adam and Eve assert their independence from God and show their lack of trust in God. By disobeying God's command, they assert their misplaced capacity to discern what is good for them apart from their relationship with God. The first sin is idolatry—humans reject God and try to put themselves in God's place. This broken relationship with God results in broken relationships among people and with nature. Sin against God precedes sins against other people and creation.

The renowned twentieth-century theologian Reinhold Niebuhr defined sin in relation to pride and power. Humans are both transcendent and finite. As transcendent beings made in the image of God, we are uniquely capable of freedom, creativity, and the capacity for ever greater personal and social fulfillment. As finite creatures, we must acknowledge our human limitations and the limits of nature. Sin results from excessive pride and will-to-power as we push our transcendence beyond the limits of human finitude. Inevitably, as we assert our self-interests and needs and as we exercise power with others, we are often prone to view our interests and needs as more important than they deserve to be, resulting sometimes in harm to others. Good and evil are permanent features of the human condition. The use of power produces both good and harmful results, so we ought to expect the use of power in work organizations to produce both good and harmful results.

Some feminist theologians have argued that Niebuhr's understanding of sin as pride and the misuse of power is inadequate because it is excessively male oriented and does not account for typical gender patterns in male-female relationships. Excessive and dominating self-assertion and power tend to be problematic male tendencies, especially at the expense of women. Women may need to find ways to be more self-assertive, especially in relation to men, to achieve relationships of mutuality, care, and empowerment. In sum, attention to gender differences and the structures of gender relationships are basic to an adequate Christian understanding of sin in work and economic life. Sin may sometimes show its face differently in men and women, but its many faces are all detrimental to nurturing Christian values important to our work and work organizations, such as respect and dignity, mutuality, care, relatedness, love and justice.

If sin is a permanent feature of the human condition, we must expect to find it in the workplace. Some Christians would claim that their work and work organizations are predominantly sinful. Others, at first glance, might not see sin at all. Yet if sin is an essential component of our Christian understanding of ourselves and the world, we must affirm its relevance to work and economic life. Where do we see sin in our work? Where does it reside in our jobs and in our work organizations? Do we know it when we see it? How do we confront it? How does sin weaken the functioning of an organization?

Barb Daniels feels it in racist comments and attitudes at work that disregard human dignity. She has seen it in the ways that power structures have tended to exclude women and members of minorities. Yet her faith is a resource, giving her the hope, energy, and courage to confront sin effectively, even to the point of loving her enemy. She works for change instead of running away.

George Bremer sees sin in an uncaring and unsupportive manager who refuses to actively and effectively motivate his workers and listen to their concerns and suggestions for improvement. He sees it in the occasional worker who exerts minimal effort and who seeks to poison the morale of a work group by perpetuating rumors, half-truths, and utter lies about other workers.

GRACE

For the person is justified and saved, not by works or laws, but by the Word of God, that is, by the promise of his grace, and by faith, that the glory may remain God's, who saved us not by works of righteousness which we may have done, but by virtue of his mercy by the word of his grace when we believed.

(Luther, "The Freedom of a Christian")

Humans, unable to satisfy God's requirements of righteousness (the demands of the law), stand before God, undeserving of salvation. Yet God provides another means for our salvation—Jesus Christ, whose perfect obedience to God's will becomes available to us through Jesus' self-sacrifice on our behalf. Our only theological requirement for righteousness becomes faith—faith in Jesus Christ that *his* righteousness can be imputed to us as well. God's acceptance of our, faith, not our works, is a gracious act. God gives us something we do not deserve—righteousness and salvation. In "The Freedom of a Christian," Luther writes, "God has given me in Christ all the riches of right-teousness and salvation without any merit on my part, out of pure, free mercy, so that from now on I need nothing except faith which believes that this is true." As a result of God's overwhelming abundance, the life of the redeemed Christian likewise becomes one of abundant giving (love and justice) toward the good of others. Luther adds, "Behold, from faith thus flow forth love and joy in the Lord, and from love a joyful, willing, and free mind that serves one's neighbor willingly."

As Christians in the workplace, do we feel that our actions at work are a response of gratitude for God's merciful acceptance of our broken lives? Do we see our actions as workers as part and parcel of our faith? Do our actions flow from our faith, or do they feel disconnected from our faith or even opposed to it? Just as we can ask ourselves where we see sin in our work organizations, so we can ask ourselves where we see glimpses of divine grace within the same institutions. To what extent do our workplaces offer gracious opportunities for us to express a life of faith active in love, justice, and service to others? And to what extent do they feel as if they inhibit that connection?

HUMAN DIGNITY

God said, "Let us make humankind in our image, according to our likeness." (Gen. 1:26)

Human dignity, focusing on the value of the person, is a centerpiece of Christian ethics. Because humans are created in the image of God, we are given special value and importance among all creatures. Our unique likeness to the Creator provides the sacred foundation for claiming that all persons are endowed with intrinsic dignity. This sacredness of human life carries obligations for how we treat others. All human relationships must aim to enhance dignity or at least not to wrongly diminish or violate another's dignity or our own.

Within the workplace, how can we respect the dignity of all persons? To some extent, human dignity requires us to show care and respect for all, regardless of rank, contribution, or importance to the organization. Yet to what extent does human dignity also require us to treat people differently, based on rank, contribution, or importance? How do we institutionalize human dignity in the structures, policies, rules, and procedures that shape personal actions within a work organization? This is no easy task. We will return to these questions in chapter 5.

LOVE AND JUSTICE

He has told you, O mortal, what is good;
    and what does the LORD require of you
but to do justice, and to love kindness,
    and to walk humbly with your God? (Mic. 6:8)

"Teacher, which commandment in the law is the greatest?" He [Jesus] said to him, " 'You shall love the Lord your God with all your heart, and with all your soul, and with all your mind.' This is the greatest and first commandment. And a second is like it: 'You shall love your neighbor as yourself.' On these two commandments hang all the law and the prophets." (Matt. 22:36-40)

If we affirm the Christian's vocation to serve the neighbor and the community (both human and nonhuman), then love and justice can be the norms specifying what this service might mean and require in practice.

What love and justice mean and how they should be applied to our lives are matters of intense, ongoing theological ethical debate. Christians must seek to discern the meaning of the word of God afresh in our lives through Scripture, theology, and human experience.

What does it mean "to do justice, and to love kindness," in the workplace? Can we do both and survive? Must we choose one or the other? Or is there a place for neither in the oftentimes tough, competitive world of business where interests and aims can clash? Are we naive to think that Christians ought to embody love and justice in situations where others do not?

We can look to the life and teachings of Jesus for meanings of Christian love and its implications for our lives. Jesus' life provided a model of *agape*—selfless, self-sacrificial love to serve the good of the neighbor, even at the expense of one's own needs. The vision of love was boundless and unconditional. Jesus demonstrated and preached compassion for sinners, outcasts, socially unacceptable people, and weak and ill people. His life can be seen as a reflection of God's boundless and unconditional love for humanity. That Jesus' love is unequivocally selfless and sacrificial is poignantly and passionately illustrated in his death on the cross for the sake of our salvation.

To what extent is this example of selfless unconditional love applicable to the Christian life? Most of us can recall personal experiences of compassionate, selfless, and unconditional love—experiences from intimate personal relationships and friendships, parent-child relationships, marriage and family life. Altruistic acts of heroism, even resulting in death for the sake of others, can stand out as poignant examples.

But can love fully and realistically be embodied within the world of work? Protestant Christian realists such as Reinhold Niebuhr have argued that love cannot be applied *directly* to the rough-and-tumble world of social institutions. Rather, love, whose aim is the good of the neighbor, must seek its impact *indirectly* through justice. Love, which seeks the good of the neighbor unconditionally, must be translated into justice, which also seeks the good of the neighbor, but conditionally. In the "real" world, love confronts the reality of sin and evil and the existence of competing claims and counterclaims. Unconditional responses, even preferential treatment, become increasingly difficult and morally problematic when the well-being of people must be managed within groups whose members are competing for scarce resources. Even the parent with more than one child quickly faces the need to distribute and allocate love and care in a way that the children perceive as fair. When we try to love unconditionally, we face the restraints of justice as fairness. Likewise, the manager who wishes to enhance the well-being of his or her organization and employees is faced with the need to allocate financial and nonfinancial goods (e.g., compensation, bonuses, titles, professional opportunities, promotions, praise and blame) not unconditionally, but conditionally, in ways that all relevant parties perceive as fair.

Living out our vocation at work—aiming to serve the good of the neighbor—requires that we practice justice. Preferential treatment, on an individual level, can become a professional liability for those who wield power. When members of a group are treated unfairly in relation to each other, they tend to become resentful and even angry, which often harms their personal productivity and the group's effectiveness as a team. Even the perception of unfairness can have harmful effects, given our egoistic tendency sometimes to perceive ourselves to be mistreated or underappreciated in relation to others, although this may not be the case at all.

The meaning of justice has been subject to great debate throughout Christian history, a debate whose many nuances lie far beyond the scope of this book. But I can highlight some basic understandings of justice within the Christian tradition so that you can consider how these notions might inform your Christian identity and apply to your world of work. We should not necessarily assume they are completely different from non-Christian understandings of justice. Christianity did not emerge and develop in a cultural vacuum. It has always been influenced by ideas, systems of thought, practices, and institutions of the societies within which it has found itself.

Justice as Fairness. Justice requires that we treat people fairly. This notion is deeply rooted within Western systems of philosophy and law, was prominent within Greek philosophy, and is well developed within the modern Western liberal philosophical tradition. Within Christianity, it receives support from the concept of human dignity. Human beings, created in the image of God, are sacred and thus deserve to be treated justly. For many, justice as fairness means treating equals equally. Discrimination and unfairness entail treating equals unequally or using inappropriate criteria to determine differences of treatment. Hence, if skin color and gender are deemed inappropriate factors on which to base compensation, then we must conclude that it is unjust and discriminatory to pay persons of color and women less money than whites and men, all other factors being equal, when they do the same work. We are treating equals unequally if the only relevant factors defining equality are such things as competence and performance. For the

Christian who affirms the sacredness of all persons created in the image of God, justice as fairness must include the conviction that racism and sexism are morally wrong and contrary to God's intentions for the world.

Consistent with the concept of justice is the affirmation of human rights. Human rights protect the individual and specify the social goods necessary for human development and flourishing. These rights typically include political rights such as free association, political participation, privacy, and due process as well as economic rights such as private property, minimal levels of economic welfare and, some would argue, employment. What counts as a moral right is subject to debate and disagreement, not only among Christians but among all citizens within a civil society.

Justice as Equality. Justice as equality asserts that persons should be treated equally with respect to important social goods. Yet we can disagree when identifying these relevant social goods. They might include material goods such as a minimal level of income, food, shelter, and education. Justice is measured more in terms of social outcomes or entitlements (who ends up with what) than in terms of fair procedures (making sure the rules of the game are fair without much concern for its outcomes).

Justice as equality asserts that human beings fundamentally are more equal than unequal. The morally relevant features that are the measuring sticks of justice are more common than unique among people. As Christians, we might say that our common identity as children of God, created by God in God's image, is the moral foundation for claiming that people have equal entitlements to at least some social goods, regardless of our condition (race, gender, class) or contribution.

Within the United States and many other Western societies, justice as equality gets embodied in our commitment to public education. It has been a long-held, deeply embedded value within our national heritage that each person deserves a good education, at least at the primary and secondary levels, and that public education should provide this social good to all irrespective of social background. For many, a strong public educational system has had a valuable leveling influence on society; it has brought people out of poverty and provided social opportunity. Our society still seems to affirm this value, and many people have benefited immensely from public education; however, the unfortunate reality for many seems to be otherwise. The quality of public education today varies greatly and has ceased miserably to fulfill its mission for millions of our nation's children, especially urban children from low-income families. And new national debates and experiments with choice in education raise the question of whether the entire public education system needs to be overhauled.

Within society and the workplace, justice as equality can be seen in the moral question of whether all persons ought to receive at least minimally adequate levels of health care coverage. Such a universal benefit would be based not on individual performance and contribution at work, which vary dramatically from person to person, but on the more basic fact that all persons have health care needs that must be met to sustain health and well-being.

Justice as Participation. Justice as participation affirms the inherently social dimension of human nature. Individuals are born as the result of a profoundly social act. As children, we survive and develop through the many relationships of dependence and mutuality with parents, relatives, neighbors, friends, teachers, and others. Persons develop and flourish primarily in relation to others through the many webs of relationships that we both choose and do not choose—family, friends, political associations, economic associations, community and voluntary organizations. And our understandings of justice must be defined in terms of these many relationships.

The U.S. Catholic bishops assert that "human dignity can be realized and protected only in community." Because participation in society is so vital to human dignity and development, they go on to assert that "all people have a right to participate in the economic life of society. Basic justice demands that people be assured a minimum level of participation in the economy" (*Economic Justice for All*, #14, #15). For the bishops, claiming the vision and language of faith means envisioning and working toward the creation of a national (and international) economy whose institutions, rules, and practices permit the healthy participation of all members of the global society. This challenge therefore points to eliminating all barriers that prevent marginalized persons, poor persons, and all persons outside the mainstream of society from having adequate access to opportunities, institutions, practices, and goods that constitute social life.

ECOLOGY AND THE COMMON GOOD

One important legacy of Roman Catholic ethics is the concept of the common good (most strongly developed within the natural law tradition whose classic spokesperson was Thomas Aquinas, joined by Jacques Maritain in the twentieth century). Persons are said to be "ordained to God" as our ultimate end. Each person is related to an infinitely great good—the common good, which is God, the divine transcendent whole. All our actions should serve this ultimate goal of human union with God. Of the goods that we seek, some are common and some are private. Common goods are social and relational. They are intrinsically good— good in themselves. Private goods are instrumentally good—

for the sake of something else. They are appropriate but only in their place when they are subservient to the common good of humanity and the universe. Most economic goods are considered private and instrumental—money, commodities, and perhaps most services. They are good not in themselves but only for the sake of other things. Food sustains life. Too much food fosters gluttony and ill health. Money sustains human well-being by securing other things necessary for life—housing, clothing, education. Too much money can encourage greed, extravagant consumption, and self-absorption.

Human beings are social; we need each other for personal development and human flourishing. Society is thus indispensable to the realization of human dignity. The proper goal of society is the good of the community, which is neither the mere collection of private goods of individuals nor the mere good of the totality irrespective of the well-being of each person. It is the good of the whole *and* of its parts. It is the "good human life of the multitude, a multitude of persons." It includes respect for essential individual human rights but also asserts that persons should direct themselves toward goods greater than themselves—to the good of the neighbor, society, and the earth, and to God. The common good includes all social goods that help each person to reach self-actualization and perfection.

The concept of the common good provides a way for Christians to chart a course between two dangerous extremes of twentieth-century social philosophy—totalitarianism and radical individualism. Totalitarianism, now finally fading from the world scene, asserted the primacy of society over the individual, permitting the violation and abuse of persons. Radical individualism asserts the primacy of the individual over society in a way that makes many social activities suspect and that understands the common good as a vacuous concept. Virtually all restraints on human freedom are deemed coercive and inappropriate. Instead, the tradition of the common good asserts the primacy of the person and his or her dignity and rights as well as our social nature to be a part of a greater whole and our destiny to seek ends greater than ourselves. Society is more than a collection of individual goods, interests, and personal preferences. It is also more than an unstable collection of special interests, with each group vying to claim its own piece of the pie. Rather, in the rightly ordered society (and ecosystem), the parts function together for the larger good of the whole—the common good of society, the cosmos, and the divine good—God.

The concept of the common good provides insights for understanding the purpose of economic life and work organizations. Economic life is inherently good insofar as it produces goods and services vital to personal and social well-being and to the common good. Yet its moral role must be put in proper perspective in the rightly ordered society. Economic activity is not supremely important insofar as the goods and services it produces are only instrumentally good. We live not for money or food or commodities or any other economic output. Yet these goods are valuable insofar as they are necessary for attaining higher ends—relationships of family, friends, political and civic associations—and the common good of society and nature. The economy cannot be an end in itself. Rather, to use the words of the U.S. Catholic bishops, "the economy is a human reality: men and women working together to develop and care for the whole of God's creation" (*Economic Justice for All*).

Yet we must not trivialize or downplay the role of economic institutions by claiming that their only role is to produce material goods—goods that are private and instrumental and, as such, less valuable or important than other intrinsic goods such as family and civic associations. Economic activity and business organizations almost always do more than create tangible private goods. For most people, our work roles and organizations also create vital relationships and purposes that define our identities and shape our lives for better or for worse. We are not merely producers of goods, we are participants in work communities whose value can be partially measured by the quality of their relationships. Businesses create organizational structures that bear down on us and shape our relationships, behavior, and actions. For some, the quality of the structured relationships is good, and it fosters personal growth and development, nurtures skills, abilities, and virtues, and links us creatively to other persons in ways that stimulate teamwork and productive teamwork. For others, the quality of the relationships is poor, and it discourages personal growth and creates disharmony, ill will, and poorly functioning and frustrating group interactions. In other words, work organizations should perform a dual function—to produce not only *tangible* (and sometimes intangible) goods and services but also *associational* goods—human relationships and personal development—which are also vital to life.

In its broadest perspective, the common good should be understood as a good for all of creation. In this sense, the common good must be viewed ecologically, striving toward the good of all life, not merely human life. The common good must aim at humanity's harmony with nature. We must judge our actions by their effects on ourselves and other people, on other species, and on the larger ecosystems in which we are participants. We shall return to this topic in chapter 5 when we discuss the impact of economic life on the natural environment.

CONCLUSION

I have highlighted some of Christianity's most fundamental theological and ethical concepts and values. Although they do not present a complete picture of the Christian moral life, they can be theological road markers for helping us to build ethical bridges between our Christian identity and our work lives. They are pieces of a puzzle that each of us must strive to assemble into a coherent vision and language of faith applicable to our work. To the challenging and sometimes ambiguous task of translating our vision and language of faith into action we must now turn our attention in the next chapter.

QUESTIONS FOR GROUP STUDY AND DISCUSSION

1. How do you react to these theological concepts and ideas?

2. Which ones seem central to your religious tradition and denomination?

3. Which concepts seem especially important to your personal identity as a Christian?

4. Which concepts seem especially challenging to live out and apply in the workplace? Do any seem to be at odds with our economic system or especially difficult to apply in your workplace?

5. What additional concepts and ideas of the Christian faith do you find important to your identity as a Christian? What additional concepts do you think should be included in a Christian ethic at work?

6. Discuss an ethical situation at work that you think was handled well from a Christian ethical perspective.

7. Discuss an ethical situation at work that you think was handled poorly from a Christian ethical perspective.

KEY RESOURCES

John Paul II. *Centesimus Annus* (papal encyclical). 1991.

Lebacqz, Karen. *Six Theories of Justice: Perspectives from Philosophical and Theological Ethics.* Minneapolis: Augsburg, 1986.

Luther, Martin. "The Freedom of a Christian." In *Martin Luther: Selections from His Writings,* edited by John Dillenberger, 42-85. New York: Doubleday, 1958.

Maritain, Jacques. *The Person and the Common Good.* Notre Dame, Ind.: University of Notre Dame Press, 1972.

Nash, James A. *Loving Nature: Ecological Integrity and Christian Responsibility.* Nashville: Abingdon Press, 1991.

Niebuhr, Reinhold. *The Nature and Destiny of Man.* 2 vols. New York: Charles Scribner's Sons, 1941–43.

Rawls, John. *A Theory of Justice.* Cambridge: Harvard University Press, 1971.

U.S. Catholic Bishops. *Economic Justice for All: Pastoral Letter on Catholic Social Teaching and the U.S. Economy.* National Conference of Catholic Bishops, 1986.

CHAPTER FOUR

Christian Ethics at Work

Translating Vision into Action

I N THE LAST CHAPTER, we discussed some classic ethical concepts of Scripture and theological traditions of the Christian faith. Their language is explicitly religious, a language that may sound out of place within business and economic life. Don't we sometimes feel that we really do live in two worlds, with different languages, values, cultures, and expectations for how we are to act and behave? Our twin communities of church and work sometimes appear to be miles apart.

Recall a typical moment in the pew at your church and the unique language of Scripture, liturgy, hymns, and songs. Recall as well a typical day at your workplace and the language and styles of communication you use there—in reports, at meetings, in conversations with coworkers, customers, or clients. Within one community, you speak and hear the language of prophets, confession, biblical narratives, ethical exhortation, hymns of joy and praise, salvation and the kingdom of God. Within the other, you might speak and hear the language of strategic goals and objectives, economic forecasts, debits and credits, sales targets, legal contracts, management philosophies and strategies, new products and services, production deadlines, cost cutting and budget reductions.

It is no wonder that for many Christians the connections between the two communities are fuzzy and illusive, hard to grasp, or even nonexistent. I recall vividly the pastor of a Lutheran congregation in a working-class community in Chicago reflecting on the utter absence of connections between religion and work for many of his blue-collar, assembly-line church members:

> Connecting religion and work is something many of my members would never consider. For them, work is brutal, degrading, dehumanizing, and exhausting. It is something over which they feel they have no power. Rather, work is merely something for them to survive—it is a paycheck—so that they can get on to the other spheres of their life that do have some religious meaning and that do provide them with some dignity—their families, leisure activities, neighborhood involvements, and their church connections.

Translating our religious vision and language is no simple task. Rather, putting our Christian ethics to work can be very hard work, both mentally and practically. First, though, it may be helpful to clarify what this challenge does *not* involve in today's work world. It cannot involve the creation of an overtly Christian political economy or workplace. That is, we cannot require that all members of our economy or our work organization convert to Christianity, much less to one particular version of Christian belief. That may have been an option within a homogeneous, authoritarian society such as medieval Christendom, but it is neither possible nor desirable within modern, pluralistic society. Not only do we celebrate the value of religious liberty, now enshrined in law, but we affirm the reality and positive value of diversity and difference. In this sense, most Western democratic societies are different not only from premodern societies but also from other modern political experiments such as the state of Israel, which though democratic, explicitly incorporates tenets of Judaism into its constitution and calls itself a Jewish state, and some more radical movements within Islam, which aim to make secular governments into explicitly Islamic states, adhering directly to tenets within the sacred scriptures of the Koran.

It we are to Christianize the workplace and economic life, it will not be through directly imposing Christian beliefs on social structures or organizations. Rather, it will occur largely to the extent that we embody Christian values through our actions and behavior in our workplace. And it will occur to the extent that we can argue persuasively and noncoercively that certain values consistent with our faith are worthy of being infused into the cultures, policies, and practices of organizations. In many cases, we will have to defend our Christian values with arguments that are not explicitly Christian but in ways that make sense to non-Christians who view the world from the perspective of other religious traditions and also to people who are not religious at all. This translation process assumes that there are ethical points of contact among religious traditions and between Christians and non-believers.

In a sense, Christians at work must be bilingual. We must be literate in the language of faith, Scripture, and theology— we must have some religious vision for our lives and the world (our discussion in the last chapter). We must also have some sense of the world of work and economic life in its own terms (our discussion in chapter 2). Yet how do we bridge the two? George Bremer, Byron Newcomb, and Barb Daniels do it in different ways on a daily basis. How do *we* become effective translators? We must now turn our attention to this task.

In this chapter, I outline several benchmarks or challenging factors that we must take into account as we put our vision into action and translate the language and values of faith in ways relevant for our work. These factors include (1) the fact of complexity and change in modern economic life, (2) the challenge of discerning the ethical relevance of Christian Scripture and theology for our lives and work today, (3) the results-oriented nature of work and business, (4) the discernment of the "more or less" of ethical action, (5) the complexity of workplace roles and the ambiguity of power within organizations, and (6) the need to view organizations as moral communities. All of these challenges can shape the ways in which we act ethically and make ethical decisions at work. Taking account of them more fully and explicitly can help us find more effective ways to make ethical connections between our faith and our work. I conclude by applying these benchmarks to a hypothetical test case—a workforce reduction situation that George Bremer must face.

COMPLEXITY AND CHANGE IN MODERN ECONOMIC LIFE

As I argued in chapter 2, economic life is immensely complex and changing rapidly. It is so multifaceted that our vision will always be partial and fragmentary. Our aim cannot be to see the whole picture but at best to catch ever-larger glimpses of the pieces that make up the whole from the perspective of our unique experiences, life histories, and areas of professional competence. For instance, impoverished Brazilians may see the global economy differently from affluent North Americans. Women may tend to see things differently from men; managers differently from employees; employees of large global companies differently from entrepreneurs of small family firms. We may see different things; and we may see the same things differently. The laid-off factory worker's experience of a plant closing may be radically different from his or her manager's experience of the same event. These differences of perspective may seem obvious, yet they cannot be ignored, for they often shape our ethical decision making and judgments in decisive ways.

Not only is economic life complex, it is also changing constantly. The global market economy today is a moving target hard to focus in our ethical sights. The moral choices we make today may be inappropriate and antiquated five or ten years from now. Some work organizations and the roles that we play within them will be so radically different in ten years that we will need to rethink completely our moral judgments about them. These changes only complicate living out a Christian ethic at work. Acknowledging this rate of change requires that we try to keep abreast of these changes and be ready and willing to revise our moral judgments about work and economic life on an ongoing basis.

DISCERNING THE ETHICAL RELEVANCE OF SCRIPTURE AND THEOLOGY FOR ECONOMIC LIFE TODAY

Modern economic life has changed radically from the places and times in which Hebrew and Christian scriptures were set. This obvious fact has a profound implication for how we try to link our Christian faith and ethics to work and economic life. For instance, Scripture says nothing about modern technologies, insider trading, labor unions, workforce reductions, and plant closings because these are unique aspects of our modern industrial-technological society. Yet Jane Corey and Mark O'Grady think that their religious traditions provide ethical resources for making moral judgments about such complex economic issues. And they hope that their parishioners will struggle to forge such connections in their lives.

How, then, do we connect the moral dimensions of age-old biblical stories and living Christian traditions to new economic situations? Some Christians believe the translation process is quite easy. Biblical literalists, for instance, might say that Scripture's inerrancy means that the Bible is a complete blueprint for ethical behavior today. We need only to identify the scriptural passage relevant to our situation and apply it literally and directly. At the other end of the spectrum, others would argue that the ethics of Christian Scriptures cannot be applied to modern social realities at all. The ethical prescriptions of the New Testament, for instance, applied to a unique early Christian community in a totally different social world. The community was expecting the imminent second coming of Christ and the emergence of a new heaven and earth unlike their existing reality. As such, the ethics of the New Testament were arguably not intended for the construction of enduring social institutions and practices.

My position lies between these two extremes. I reject the biblical literalist's tendency to make quick, easy, and unambiguous moral connections between scriptural passages and contemporary life experiences. I reject the relativist's tendency to discount too quickly the extent to which Scripture and tradition reveal and disclose *enduring* truths about who we are and how we ought to live. Rather, I believe that general ethical themes, ideals, and values mediate between the centuries-old language of Scripture and the complex world of modern work. Identifying these mediating themes—and figuring out how to apply them to our lives—is a creative, interpretive process.

For the most part, Christian ethics at work is not an easy application of moral rules that can be lifted from Scripture and then clearly and unambiguously applied to each and every situation. Jesus did not provide many detailed rules on what to do in our lives. "Love your neighbor as yourself" is very general. We have the responsibility to determine what it means concretely in our lives. Rather, most detailed ethical rules are provisional and evolving, as wisdom and situations change. For instance, medieval theologians condemned taking interest on loans. We have changed our ethical thinking on this issue for good reasons. Yet we can also appeal to enduring norms and principles from Scripture. The commandment "Do not steal" from the Decalogue is an enduring principle that can be applied in work situations fairly unambiguously. Yet in some narrowly defined situations, stealing has been argued to be morally permissible (for example, in cases where starvation is imminent and a greater good is at stake—the preservation of human life itself).

Let's consider a complex contemporary moral issue—insider trading. We can say that insider trading is wrong from a Christian perspective because it violates the commandment "Do not steal." It constitutes an act of injustice; the offender takes something that is rightfully (and legally) another's. It is a violation of a human right and of human dignity. But even what most would see as an easy moral issue to analyze from a Christian ethical perspective quickly becomes complicated when we try to define insider trading with precision. It is not always clear what is public information (which can be shared freely and without moral censure) and what is inside or private information (which cannot be shared freely and whose inappropriate use is the basis of insider trading). In sum, because there is no clear and comprehensive Christian ethical blueprint for modern business and economic life, we must accept that translating our Christian visions and values into action in the workplace will be a creative and sometimes open-ended, intuitive, imperfect, and even ambiguous enterprise.

As I illustrated in the previous chapter, one primary way we bridge the gap between faith and work is to lift out classic theological and ethical concepts and ideas from Scripture and our living, historical traditions and then creatively attempt to infer and discern their meanings and applications for our lives. This approach is akin to values-based management. Our aim is to identify the key values and ideals that we wish to drive and guide our actions, both as individuals and as institutions.

Christian values and norms do not hover in the sky above us as if they are some abstract, disembodied, unchanging, uniformly understood set of truths that each age needs merely to pluck down and apply to its situation. Rather, these values are shaped by the larger societies in which we live and by events that we experience as individuals and as societies. For instance, the ways that many North Americans, including Christians, understand concepts such as social equality and equal opportunity have been vividly shaped and reshaped by the civil rights movement of the fifties and sixties; the movement forced the entire nation to confront the painful realities of racism in ways that it had previously ignored. Or consider the example of smoking in the workplace. Twenty years ago, many people would have said that the right to freedom means that our right to smoke in the workplace should be respected and protected. Now we appeal to the same value of freedom but say that others have the right to breathe clean air (to be protected from the harms of secondary smoke). The direction of influence here is not unidirectional but is reciprocal. Christian values and norms shape the ways that we live our lives and construct social institutions; social experiences shape the ways in which we interpret the meanings of these values and norms.

THE RESULTS-ORIENTED NATURE OF BUSINESS AND WORK

Christian values and norms are not the only values and norms at work in society and in the workplace. As some have argued (such as John Atherton), the market generates its own social values and civic virtues. A third benchmark for a Christian ethic at work, then, is to acknowledge the special purposes and practical nature of work and modern work organizations, and the values and norms that support these purposes.

By necessity, business is results oriented. Business organizations function for specific purposes—the production of goods and services offered in exchange for money. People who work within organizations have discrete and measurable tasks. If we are to put a Christian ethic to work, it must help persons make choices that advance the purposes of the organization. It must relate to the concrete tasks, pressures, and objectives associated with our occupations and job responsibilities. And it must also relate somehow to the economic and organizational values within our market economic system and institutions. Such values include efficiency, productivity, flexibility, and teamwork.

When we ask, "What does it mean to be an effective manager or employee?" we might appeal to various values and norms such as the ones mentioned above. They might include hard work, self-discipline, the capacity to solve problems, the ability to get along well with others and/or to manage others, high levels of intelligence, appropriate competence in one's field or technical area, honesty, and trustworthiness. Although some of these values might be explicit or implicit Christian values, many are not, but are generated from within contemporary economic life itself.

When we ask, "What does it mean to be an effective *Christian* manager or employee?" we can also appeal to a second layer of *Christian* values and norms, such as love, justice, dignity, and stewardship. But Christian theology and ethics are not sufficient sources of values to determine what it is to be an effective Christian *manager* or *employee* in today's market economy. For instance, a good Christian engineer who desires to build bridges must be more than a good Christian. He or she must also be a good engineer who knows how to build bridges well according to the most up-to-date technological knowledge within the field of civil engineering. At the same time, though, one's identity as a Christian might enhance one's professional identity and capacities as an engineer. And as a Christian engineer, one would be concerned with the larger social purposes of a bridge as well as its environmental impacts.

A theological ethic for business and economic life must be practical. It must provoke thoughtful reflection about what we do; it must affect and shape our choices and provide directions for our actions. As we move into positions of greater responsibility within organizations, we assume more and more power and are required to make decisions and judgments that have larger and wider impacts on others. Unfortunately, this heightened responsibility rarely comes with the additional time that we might wish in order to reflect fully and carefully about each decision. Instead, executives are usually expected to make judgments quickly and efficiently, often under intense pressure and with limited information. Organizations rarely stop so that we can reflect and make judgments about their future well-being.

Without the luxury of time, executives and managers often are required to make decisions on the spot. For a senior executive like George Bremer who is faced with the mandate to reduce his workforce by 10 percent within sixty days, Christian ethics must inform his deliberations, planning, and strategies and tactics for action quickly and proactively, perhaps even instinctively. For Byron Newcomb, his Christian ethics must help him decide whether or not his ad agency should take on a new corporate client, based in part on moral judgments he must make about the appropriateness of the potential client's products. For Barb Daniels, it means struggling to determine, on what seems like a nearly daily basis, how to survive, perform well, and get ahead in a predominantly white and male workplace. These individuals cannot escape these issues, which their positions require them to confront and resolve regularly and effectively. In coping with these kinds of issues, Christians will find their faith to be vital and relevant or impractical and irrelevant.

A Christian ethic at work must help us assess the outcomes, goals, and objectives that we are responsible to attain at work both individually and corporately; it must also help us assess the means for getting there. We must ask ourselves whether the organization's objectives and values cohere with the values of our Christian faith. The ends do not necessarily justify the means. *How* we accomplish work objectives is also relevant to our Christian faith. We may sometimes conclude that work objectives are not worth pursuing if we must compromise too much ethically to get there. To say that a Christian ethic at work should be practical and help us make effective workplace choices and decisions is not to say that we should always expect to find perfect harmony between Christian values and workplace goals and values. Norms such as justice and human dignity, and the realities of sin and evil in the world, may cause us to denounce and to reject some economic decisions, policies, and practices. On occasion, we will be compelled to say no.

ETHICS AS THE ART OF THE POSSIBLE: DISCERNING THE "MORE OR LESS" OF ETHICAL ACTION

In a theological sense, we can never fully succeed at living out Christian ethical values and ideals. If we take sin seriously as a fundamental aspect of the human condition, we know that we cannot achieve perfection, individually or organizationally. In this sense, we affirm Luther's emphasis on the Pauline truth that we can be justified by faith, not by works. Christians are called to do good works and obey the moral law, yet we remain sinners. Whatever our ethical achievements, be they noble, hard-won, and life-giving, they will nevertheless remain partial, imperfect, flawed, and subject both to renewal and to disintegration. Though our faith compels us to seek the highest of our ethical ideals—love, justice, dignity, the common good—we cannot expect perfection from ourselves, other persons, or the organizations in which we participate.

Our faith should transform our lives. Christians ought to strive to transform the world around us. But our efforts are always limited by our imperfection and by the inherent constraints placed on our powers to act. Ethical action is rarely an "all or nothing" choice between moral perfection on the one hand and total moral depravity on the other. This is usually true with regard to the choices available to us within our work organizations. For example, the choice is rarely, if ever, between total and absolute justice and the total absence of justice. Rather, organizations are always more or less just and more or less fair, and we are usually after the incremental "more." Barb Daniels knows she will not see racism disappear overnight. She feels the pain of continued acts of exclusion, but she celebrates the gains she has seen over the last ten years for herself, other minority persons in her organization, and the organization itself as it becomes a more effective, productive, and humane workplace.

Our faith may compel us strongly and deeply to condemn and denounce all forms of injustice, such as racism and sexism; however, it does not also necessarily tell us to reject our organizations because they have racist or sexist practices. Naming social practices as racist or sexist should compel us in most cases to minimize (and in rare and gracious instances to eliminate) these practices within ourselves, other persons, or organizations. But in most cases, the change that we can effect is incremental and not absolute. Byron Newcomb cannot eliminate all violence and sexism in advertising in our country, but he can work with his clients to convince them not to use violent or sexist images in their advertisements. The justice and the fairness that we seek within relationships and organizations are partial, subject to improvements and progress, and to deterioration and decay. What we usually seek when we attempt to put our Christian faith to work can be measured incrementally by the "more or less" of our fundamental moral values. Our choices are usually incremental and strategic, aiming to create measurable change, but recognizing that our power to act is usually constrained by many factors. As the theological ethicist James Gustafson observes,

> There are morally conscientious persons, many of them with deep Christian convictions, whose positions of responsibility require them to make choices and engage in actions limited by economic, social, political, medical, and legal realities. For them, if not the first question, one of the first questions is "What is possible within the circumstances, the resources, the competing claims, in which I act?" Multinational corporations may appear to be the root of much injustice to many Christian prophets, and they like to condemn such businesses. But that condemnation is of no moral assistance to a responsible executive in such a corporation, who seeks to direct its powers toward the public good. ("Varieties of Moral Discourse")

If, for instance, we seek to place appropriate numbers of outstanding, highly qualified women and minority persons into leadership positions within a large organization that is predominantly white male, that ethical goal cannot happen overnight. With appropriate organizational commitments, leadership, goals, planning, training, and hard work, though, change can occur. Although complacency can never be justified as long as vestiges of racism and sexism exist, as Christians, we can celebrate the partial victories of incremental change as we move toward our ethical goal. In an imperfect and broken world, the actual and partial "more or less" approximations of ethical ideals make a significant difference.

THE COMPLEXITY OF WORKPLACE ROLES AND THE AMBIGUITY OF POWER WITHIN ORGANIZATIONS

Being Christians in the world today is a challenge regardless of where we work. It is especially challenging in light of the global economy and increasing change within work organizations. How we see ourselves, how we define our roles and expectations, how we conduct ourselves, and how we make decisions as Christians at work are shaped by a myriad of factors, some of which we are very aware, some only faintly aware, and some often completely unaware. The kind of organization for which we work, its purpose, structure, and culture; the position we hold in the organization; the personality of the individual for whom we work and our unique relationship with her or him; the quality of our interactions with coworkers; how well we like or dislike our work—all of these factors shape the concrete ways in which we see our workplace roles. And it is within these discrete social roles that we struggle to be Christians at work, to embody our faith and our ethics in our actions and decisions.

These workplace roles, and the many social, organizational, and interpersonal factors that shape them, provide both possibilities and constraints for living out our faith at work. Whether chief executive officer, general manager, accountant, junior manager, or office secretary, the role at work presents opportunities to act within a web of relationships and a sphere of influence that would otherwise be closed to us. And the same structures that bear down on us to shape our roles constrain or limit what we can do as Christians at work. For some, the sphere of influence is considerable; for others, the capacity to act may seem so restrained as to make us feel utterly powerless.

For instance, if I work for an organization with a poor track record of hiring, retaining, and promoting women, and I have been hired recently into an entry-level professional position, I may conclude that I have virtually no power (or authority) yet to raise this concern and/or attempt to work for change within the organization. My current position is a constraint on my capacity to act and respond to what I think is an organizational problem. But if I am CEO, I certainly have power and authority to address the issue. We might argue that my CEO role not only provides the *possibility* for moral action but also carries with it an *obligation* of stewardship and justice to address issues such as men's and women's roles within my organization.

The more challenging question, though, is how the rest of us address ethical issues, for most of us are neither CEOs nor new entry-level employees. We might say that new hires don't have much power and responsibility to address an organizational ethical issue. And we can say a CEO should. But we cannot throw responsibility for all of an organization's ethical issues only into the lap of the CEO or another senior manager. At some point, we must ask whether and to what extent we personally should feel morally compelled to exercise responsibility for an ethical issue. At this point, Christian ethics becomes the art of the possible as we intuitively attempt to measure our choices and strategies in terms of how our workplace roles provide both possibilities and constraints for action. Are the constraints so decisive that they overwhelm my capacity to make a difference in addressing an issue? Or are there creative ways that I might overcome my constraints and create new possibilities for moral response? And how can I convince others within my organization to try to make a difference with me?

Any Christian ethic at work must come to grips with power and its uses. The exercise of power is inevitable. Humans exhibit power over nature. We exhibit power with each other. Power comes into play in each and every human relationship. Power involves the ways in which we exert influence over others, be they people or nature. Some have defined power as the capacity to overcome resistance and/or constraints to get others to do what we want. This is a morally neutral definition, for it says nothing about whether the things we might want others to do are good or bad.

The use of power is not only inevitable; it is also morally ambiguous. Power can be used to obtain morally appropriate and morally inappropriate goals, and it can be exercised in mutually beneficial and life-affirming ways and dominating, harmful, and even violent ways. Power can be used in ways that encourage personal growth and the strengthening of moral community; it can be wielded in ways that are manipulative and destructive of healthy relationships.

Certainly there is no single appropriate form of power. Rather, different forms are appropriate in different contexts and institutional settings. In warfare, power can be coercive and violent. Within the military, power may be appropriately authoritarian. Within parent-child relationships, it may initially be authoritarian but rightly changes form and becomes more mutual and persuasive as the child moves toward responsible adulthood. (This power shift may save the parent-child relationship itself from dissolution.) Eventually, parents can feel utterly powerless to influence their children.

Within the modern U.S. workplace, uses of power and styles of authority are undergoing a gradual process of change. Within the old management paradigm, modeled on highly efficient military organizations, power tended to be authoritarian and wielded within highly centralized organizational hierarchies. Power was unidirectional. Bosses told their employees what to do and employees (the bosses hoped) obeyed. Decisions were made "on high." Orders were sent "through the ranks" of the organization for implementation. As businesses are responding to changes in the globally competitive business environment, they are changing their organizational structures and styles of management. As businesses have become leaner and more quickly responsive to the customer or client, they have become less hierarchical and authoritarian. Power becomes more fluid, consensual, multidirectional, and team oriented. Some suggest that these shifts in the uses and styles of power within organizations are more feminine. If true, this tendency coincides with the growing participation of women at almost all levels of the workforce, numerically and proportionally.

Christian ethics at work can be seen as a meditation on the uses and misuses of power. Power is an inherent feature of work life. As people move up the organizational ladder, they assume more and more power on behalf of the organization. Promotions and advancement, especially into managerial positions, mean the acquisition of more power. Christian faith and ethics should help us shed light on what it means to use power responsibly. To whom are we accountable as wielders of power: shareholders, bosses, fellow workers, customers or clients, local communities, suppliers, governmental bodies, the nation, the human community, the natural environment? How do Christian ethical concepts such as human dignity, stewardship, and justice shape our understandings of power and its appropriate and inappropriate uses? Businesses and other work organizations can be understood in terms of the ways that they distribute power within their organizations. Who receives power? How is it used?

Many ethical problems and issues in work organizations are the consequences of the misuse of power: the feeling of alienation among women because of sexual harassment, workforce reductions caused by mismanagement, environment degradation resulting from ignored environmental protection laws, bribes and other forms of monetary fraud. Many ethical problems can be avoided through the responsible use of power. The ethical expectations we assign to ourselves and others in the workplace depend to a great extent on the power available to us.

For George Bremer, senior executive at a large global company, his power and range of discretionary action as a

Christian at work are broader than most workers will experience. He has power to hire and fire, determine compensation within corporate guidelines, and set budgets that attempt to accomplish corporate objectives. Yet even George often feels severely constrained in what he can do by forces beyond his control—the health (or weakness) of the economy, technological innovations, competitors' actions, changing governmental regulations, corporate policies, current corporate priorities, the peculiar personality traits and interactive styles of his boss—the chief executive officer.

As a lower level manager and as an African American woman, Barb Daniels experiences her workplace and its possibilities and constraints much differently from George Bremer. Barb's power and discretionary action are much more severely restricted. Like George, she struggles to learn to do more with less when her departmental budget allocations continue to be pinched. She constantly works hard as an African American woman to interpret the signals and messages of a predominantly white male culture. She feels that she often needs to go the second mile to maintain a high-enough comfort level and rapport with her white male boss, who has had no personal experience with minority cultures. Barb struggles to know how best to adapt to a corporate culture whose values and actions she does not always believe in. She struggles to know what things to accept or ignore, and what things to push and try to change. She also works hard to keep abreast of technological and organizational change so that she and the people in her department will continue to be highly productive contributors to the organization, and not workers who risk obsolescence.

ORGANIZATIONS AS MORAL COMMUNITIES

Ethical action does not happen in a vacuum. Rarely do we make choices impervious to what is going on around us. Rather, the communities of which we are members—families, neighborhoods, levels of political community, churches, civic organizations, work organizations—shape ethical choices. Usually, our choices are meant to be fitting within these communities. Every group, organization, or institution can be understood as a moral community, each with its cultural ethos and ethical expectations. In this sense, a band of criminals is a moral community, for its members are bound together by a common purpose and some degree of (unstable) trust and reciprocity, even though their purposes are harmful to the larger society. Likewise, every work organization is a moral community with common purposes and a set of moral expectations and standards, explicit or implicit, to guide the conduct of its members. At the same time, we may think some of the purposes are unethical and some of its standards of conduct are less than ideal.

No moral community is perfect, and we ought never naively to expect that we can attain perfection. But neither must we necessarily accept its imperfections and inadequacies as givens and as intractable. Nor should we too quickly walk away from them. If the workplace is a moral community, we must ask ourselves what our commitments are to the organization. Our challenge becomes that of transformation—using our power and opportunities to embody ethical norms such as dignity and justice within our relationships and to seek ways that our organizations can better approximate such norms within their cultures, policies, and practices.

SUMMARY OF THE BENCHMARKS

I have provided a series of questions to help you use these benchmarks in thinking about your work. I will conclude by offering a short hypothetical test case of a workforce reduction situation to show how they might work in practice.

With Respect to Complexity and Change in Modern Economic Life:
- What aspects of modern economic life seem especially complicated to me?
- What aspects of economic life around me seem to be changing most rapidly? What additional changes can I anticipate over the next ten or twenty years? And what are the most dramatic changes that I have experienced in my work roles and in my work organization? How should I anticipate my work and my work organization to change most significantly in the future?

With Respect to Translating the Ethical Relevance of Scripture and Theology for My Work Life:
- What theological and ethical values and norms from Scripture and Christian tradition do I believe are most enduring and relevant today?
- How shall I weave them together into a vision of the faith that can provide me with Christian identity and direction for my life at work and within the economy?
- How do I translate their meanings and applications for my daily work activity?

With Regard to the Results-Oriented Nature of Work Organizations:
- What are the primary values that drive economic life today? What are the primary values that shape the culture and expectations of people in my organization? What are the primary values that shape the expectations of my organization regarding my work roles and tasks?
- How do the values of my Christian faith relate to these workplace values? Do my Christian values help me perform my work better? When do they conflict with the

values and expectations of my organization and create moral tension and discomfort for me?

With Regard to Ethics as the Art of the Possible:

- How do I measure success in the application of my Christian ethics at work? What counts as moral progress for me and for my organization?
- When might it be appropriate to throw in the towel? When, as a judgment of last resort, might it be appropriate to conclude that I must quit my job and leave my organization because I find my job to be sufficiently intolerable or unfulfilling or aspects of my organization's culture and practices to be morally problematic? What is my tolerance for moral ambiguity?

With Regard to the Exercise and Uses of Power:

- How much power do I have in my workplace? Do I feel powerful or powerless?
- What are the predominant ways that power is exercised in my organization (dictatorial, authoritarian, consensual, persuasive)?
- What are the most humane ways to wield power in my workplace?
- What creative possibilities for the use of power do I have that might provide opportunities for moral change and transformation within my organization?

With Regard to Organizations as Moral Communities:

- To what extent does my workplace feel like a moral community?
- What are its strongest moral features?
- Where is its moral performance weak or vulnerable and in need of strengthening?
- How might the strengthening of my work organization as a moral community enhance our performance and allow us to accomplish our mission more effectively?

MANAGING A WORKFORCE REDUCTION: A HYPOTHETICAL TEST CASE FOR CHRISTIAN ETHICS AT WORK

Forced to cut costs within his regional manufacturing facilities, George Bremer is faced with the imminent need to reduce his workforce by 10 percent. How should George make this decision as a Christian manager? What are his responsibilities as senior manager to his company, its shareholders, his employees, and others in this situation? Let's walk through the six benchmarks to see how they might help George think about this difficult problem, evaluate his options, and make a decision that he can live with and that seems defensible from a Christian perspective.

With respect to the dynamism of the market and the reality of economic change, George would want to know the reasons for the corporate directive to reduce his manufacturing costs. Is the cause external and long-term, such as technological changes that are making some of George's workers redundant and manufacturing processes obsolete? If so, can the workers be retrained to avoid obsolescence in ways that enhance their productivity and justify their cost to the business? Is the cause external but temporary, such as a downturn in the business cycle, which may be subject to imminent reversal? Is the cause internal, such as mismanagement, resulting in inefficient allocation of workers and capital? Each cause may imply a different strategic response.

With respect to theological and ethical values, George must determine what Christian values seem most relevant in this situation. Perhaps he will see the execution of his managerial role and power in terms of stewardship; then he will want to ask himself to whom is he accountable. Clearly, he is accountable directly to the CEO, to whom he reports, and indirectly to the company's shareholders, to whom management has fiduciary duties. But as a Christian steward, he is also arguably morally accountable to additional constituent groups that will be affected by his decisions, such as the company's employees and the local communities within which his facilities are located. In such a case, though, there does not seem to be a Christian ethical blueprint for sorting through and weighing the various obligations.

If George concludes that a reduction in his workforce is inevitable, due to increased global competition and technological change, he may yet invoke Christian notions of justice and human dignity in his deliberations about how best to implement the reduction. Deciding which workers to let go and what to provide them becomes a critical moral issue.

With regard to the results-oriented nature of business and the incremental nature of moral action and progress, George must consider how his Christian identity and values do or do not add value to his role as manager in his decision-making situation. Do his Christian convictions make his decision easier or more difficult? Perhaps the CEO of his company wants him to effect the workforce reduction as quickly and cost-effectively as possible, to the extent that only minimal severance payments and other forms of assistance are provided to terminated workers. If such a directive seems to conflict with George's sense of justice and human dignity, how will he express these moral convictions and consider whether to negotiate stronger severance packages? What compromise will George find morally tolerable when corporate financial resources are insufficient to provide optimal support? How much leverage does George have to negotiate the incremental "more or less" of distributive justice in this situation?

With respect to the use of power, George may wish to ask how the decision of cutting production costs can be best made. Who should be involved in deciding how to maximize benefits and minimize harm? If he has no time to involve lower levels of workers, perhaps he will conclude that he ought to develop longer-term collaborative efforts to anticipate such situations in the future, perhaps even to avert them. Can he create labor-management communication structures that can work to avoid the shock of future workforce reductions? How

might his people create ongoing worker retraining programs to minimize redundancy and sustain long-term employment? How might his company involve itself in larger
public policy debates and try to shape effective government
policies with respect to workforce reductions and plant closings?

With respect to viewing his organization as a moral community, George must be concerned with the impacts of his decision on employees who are terminated and on those who are
retained. How will the reduction in force affect future productivity and morale? Does it run the risk of reducing trust and
loyalty among his people that are crucial to high productivity
and performance? Can he craft both an *outcome* and a *process*
that are perceived as fair to his people? Are there ways that he
might use this difficult situation to strengthen the quality of
moral community within his organization in the future?

As can be seen, even in a hypothetical test case such as a
workforce reduction, simple and universally valid solutions
may not easily emerge from this method of doing Christian
ethics. Admittedly, we do not have enough facts to make a
clear judgment in this situation. Rather, what emerge are
organizing questions that can point us toward decisions and
conclusions that we hope are faithful to our Christian commitments and shaped and informed by our Christian values.

QUESTIONS FOR GROUP STUDY AND DISCUSSION

1. How do you go about translating the vision of faith into
   your life at work and in the economy?

2. What is your response to the six benchmarks for translating Christian vision into action?

3. Which of them seem most difficult or challenging?

4. Are there additional benchmarks or considerations that should be factored into Christian ethical decision making?

5. Do you find these benchmarks helpful in your efforts to respond to the most challenging ethical issues in your workplace?

6. Describe an ethical issue from your workplace, and with your study group, attempt to use some or all of the benchmarks to discern possible approaches and responses in light of our faith.

KEY RESOURCES

Atherton, John. *Christianity and the Market: Christian Social Thought for Our Times.* London: SPCK, 1992.

Gustafson, James M. "Varieties of Moral Discourse: Prophetic Narrative, Ethical, and Policy," a lecture delivered at Calvin College and Seminary, 1987.

Hart, Stephen. *What Does the Lord Require?: How American Christians Think About Economic Justice.* New York: Oxford University Press, 1992.

Hay, Donald. *Economics Today: A Christian Critique.* London: Apollos, 1989.

McCoy, Charles S. *Management of Values: The Ethical Difference in Corporate Policy and Performance.* Boston: Pitman, 1985.

Meeks, M. Douglas. *God the Economist: The Doctrine of God and Political Economy.* Philadelphia: Fortress, 1989.

Novak, Michael. *The Catholic Ethic and the Spirit of Capitalism.* New York: Free Press, 1993.

Preston, Ronald H. *Religions and the Ambiguities of Capitalism.* Cleveland: Pilgrim, 1993.

Wogaman, J. Philip. *The Great Economic Debate: An Ethical Analysis.* Philadelphia: Westminster, 1977.

CHAPTER FIVE

Critical Issues for Christians at Work

NOW THAT WE HAVE discussed some ingredients of a Christian ethic for work and economic life, let us turn our attention to five critical economic and workplace issues that will face Christians and others as we move into the twenty-first century. These issues are (1) routine, professional integrity issues and challenges, (2) the changing relationships and expectations of organizations and their workers, (3) the persistence of discrimination and the challenge of diversity within the workplace, (4) the changing roles and responsibilities of governments in relation to the economy, and (5) the ecological challenge of environmental protection and sustainability. Certainly, this list is not complete; each of us could and should add to it as we probe the meanings of our faith for our work. These five have been selected because they seem so fundamental and inescapable. They are broad and systemic, yet they will affect virtually all of us in deeply personal and practical ways. They will beg for our response at the levels of the individual, the organization, public policy and government, the economy at large, and the global community.

WORKING WITH INTEGRITY ON A DAILY BASIS

Some ethical issues at work are not new at all but provide enduring challenges for most Christians at work. I define them as basic integrity issues and challenges. We face them on an almost daily basis. No work organization is perfect, and all of us are bound to see some things about our organizations and those around us that we think are ethically problematic. Perhaps we know individuals who lie about work-related matters to cover for themselves or their work groups. Perhaps we know of or suspect an individual who steals from the organization. Perhaps we continually see an underperforming employee whose inadequate performance is covered up or ignored, causing a festering in group productivity and morale. Perhaps we see a manager who is willing to look the other way when a corporate policy or procedure is stretched because he or she stands to gain somehow from this ethical exception to the rule. Perhaps we know of a manager who abuses power by unfairly showing preference toward some in the organization. It may happen in hiring and in promotions, where standard procedures to ensure fair and equal treatment are ignored or slighted. It may happen where normal and formal channels of decision making and deliberation are skirted to influence unfairly an outcome, be it in personnel matters, purchasing, or budgeting.

These and other "minor" everyday ethical issues are not to be ignored or slighted, for they can be a part of the daily ethical reality of our work. Though not global in scope, these ethical issues can most occupy our emotional energies. They can fester in our consciousness and frustrate us when we feel unable to change them or we become directly or indirectly involved in them.

In these situations, we are challenged to identify the Christian ethical values that we think will help us discern the ethical problem and to seek an effective response to the problem. The considerations discussed in chapter 4 enter in here: "Do I have the power to make a difference or change the situation? Should I fight this battle, or save it for another day? How much change should I be satisfied with (the 'more or less' of Christian ethics)?" Responding to lapses in integrity on the part of others often requires real personal risk and courage on our part. It may also require the informal support of others in the organization and formal support of the organization.

WORK ORGANIZATIONS AND THEIR WORKERS: PRODUCTIVITY AND LOYALTY IN A DYNAMIC GLOBAL ECONOMY

During most of the post–World War II period, the U.S. economy experienced steady increases in growth and prosperity. After World War II, the U.S. economy assumed a position of unrivaled leadership, dominating world markets in virtually every manufacturing sector in which we wished to compete. This dominance was temporary, as new competitors emerged around the globe. During this period, especially in the fifties and sixties, both U.S. employment and wage levels increased steadily. For most, rising prosperity was expected. Jobs were in abundant supply. The largest U.S. corporations—GM, Ford, GE, U.S. Steel—grew rapidly to satisfy an ever-expanding domestic consumer demand and foreign markets for which there were virtually no competitors. Except for (usually temporary) layoffs generated by normal business cycles, employment for most (white) Americans was never in question. The average worker might live and die with the same company. Employment for life could be virtually expected at companies such as "Ma Bell" and General Motors. Of course, there were periods of adversarial labor-management relations. But for the most part, a psychological contract existed between the U.S. corporation and its workers. The company provided stable, long-term employment with the expectation of steadily increasing wages and benefits; the worker provided steady work with modest gains in productivity. The result was a relatively stable and predictable win-win relationship in which both parties showed at least modest levels of goodwill, commitment, and loyalty toward each other.

As we noted in chapter 2, those days seem past forever. The new reality of global competition and factors such as rapid technological change have radically challenged that old psychological contract. U.S. companies, now faced with global head-to-head competition in industry after industry, are shedding employees to reduce production costs and remain competitive. For the last decade, substantial work-force reductions have occurred at all levels of the corporation. U.S. Fortune 500 firms cut their payrolls from 16.2 million employees in 1990 to 11.8 million in mid-1993. Large U.S. companies announce plans to reduce their workforces 2 percent, 5 percent, 10 percent, even 20 percent, sometimes involving tens of thousands of workers, through natural attrition, voluntary reductions such as early retirements, but sometimes through immediate involuntary layoffs that can leave workers and local communities in shock. The other side of the story is that most new job creation in our country occurs within small businesses.

This predicament, not only in the United States but in other high-wage industrialized countries as well, is perhaps the most dramatic current example of what the economic historian Joseph Schumpeter called capitalism's "creative destruction," that is, technological change constantly creates new products and production methods, making obsolete the old. It has generated a moral dilemma. The old order provided more job stability but with lower productivity and lower quality products. The new global order has reduced job stability, at least for the present period, while generating higher demands for efficiency and productivity and higher quality products at lower cost to the consumer.

Undoubtedly, countless Americans distrust and feel bitter about this change, preferring the days when employment was more stable and virtually guaranteed long-term by the employer. Many Americans support public policy measures that would attempt to protect U.S. jobs by somehow turning back or restricting this uncertain evolutionary process that has generated pain and dislocation for many American workers.

Responsive, highly skilled, highly adaptable, highly motivated employees in a competitive global economy need higher levels of investment in continuous training and education to avoid obsolescence. Yet many corporations and other organizations, forced to cut production costs, have fewer and fewer financial resources to devote to this critical task. Even German corporations, world renowned for their highly sophisticated and formalized systems of on-the-job vocational training and skills development, are facing pressures to reduce these investments. German labor costs have increased to levels above those of other industrialized nations, causing fear of uncompetitiveness.

As Christians, we need to wrestle with the importance of loyalty as a value to be institutionalized within the work organizations of the new global economy. The moral issue hinges on the relationship between loyalty and productivity. Understanding this relationship is critical for the well-being of work organizations and the economy. It is also critical for the dignity and well-being of workers. Loyalty has *instrumental* economic value if it contributes to higher productivity. Loyalty also has *intrinsic* human value when it contributes to the sense of spiritual satisfaction and moral meaning that workers seek to gain from the workplace. As John Haughey argues, loyalties are essential to the development of persons, for they "make people live for more than themselves" ("The Growing Dilemma of Loyalty and the Firm"). Loyalties shape the self and foster individuality as well as the ability to make commitments. Loyalties generate trust by engendering respect.

Haughey goes on to argue that not all loyalties between company and employee have necessarily been good and mature:

Some loyalties are a cover camouflaging character weaknesses. Underneath the cover there are losers who have gotten by without initiative, creativity, industry, innovation. Some companies without intending such an outcome develop a culture that creates loyalists who are rewarded for their longevity instead of for those qualities necessary for a company to stay competitive. Instead of remaining lean, some companies become a stable for leaners. Leaners subtly repose the weight of their needs on the company rather than concern themselves with its productivity and profitability. ("The Growing Dilemma of Loyalty and the Firm")

What kinds of loyalties should we seek in the new global economy between work organizations and their workers? In a more dynamic economy, loyalty will be more conditional on performance and perhaps less long-term. We don't want immature loyalties of the kind described above where poor performers hide within an organization. Neither do we want the absence of loyalty, for workers are always more than mere factors of production like physical plants, technology, or financial capital. Persons ought never to be merely instruments for the sake of economic gain. Rather, we need loyalty that contributes to personal maturation as well as productivity for the organization.

Retaining a sense of loyalty in the workplace will require that we devise means to retain workers who are flexible and adaptable enough to sustain high levels of productivity over a long period. It will require strong commitments by our educational systems, public and private, to provide workers with the skills and abilities appropriate for a highly dynamic economy. It will require strong commitments by employers and managers such as George Bremer and Byron Newcomb to continuously train and retrain their workforces in cost-effective ways. It will require strong commitments by workers such as Barb Daniels to envision learning as a lifelong process and discipline in which they must continually be engaged. It will require commitments by governments to continue to provide social safety nets that can ease the sometimes painful transition accompanying the loss of a job. This last role will be advanced to the extent that persons such as Jane Corey and Mark O'Grady, as citizens and as religious leaders, voice their convictions about what they think is the proper role of government in a global economy. For many workers, it may require a change in expectations about what we think our work and our workplaces should provide us. If loyalty between worker and work organization will be less permanent in the global economy, we may need to temper our loyalties and expectations with respect to our work. This tempering may result in a fuller and more wholistic sense of self in which our loyalties—to work, family, self, church, community institutions—become more in balance with each other.

For Christians, this shift can be placed within a theological framework of meaning: our work should not become our God. In a dynamic global economy, workers will likely change jobs and employers more frequently. The positive side is that some individuals may reconsider their loyalties to work, reducing the risk of idolatry—of placing too much faith and trust in the wrong objects of value. While trying to avoid the sin of idolatry, we nevertheless want to hold on to core values such as dignity and justice in the workplace and a personal sense of vocation. Although work organizations may be more dynamic and changing, we want their policies and practices to embody our commitments to justice and fairness in the ways they treat people. And as Christians, we want to see our roles and functions in the workplace as ways of living out a sense of vocation and stewardship in an even more rapidly changing world.

DISCRIMINATION AND DIVERSITY

Unlike virtually all other countries, the United States has never defined itself primarily by ethnicity. Being an American has always meant something fundamentally different from being a member of a particular ethnic group, even though most of our early settlers came from only a handful of northern European nations. Countless immigrants have come to the United States to break free from the very ethnicities of their countries of origin. Our history is one of expanding multiculturalism and diversity.

Our history is also a saga of exclusion and discrimination. Race, sex and gender, religion, and sexual orientation have too often provided the means to include some people and exclude others. Racism has divided our nation since the first Africans were forcefully brought to our shores as slaves. It has shown its face as we pushed Native Americans westward in the wake of the expansion of Anglo settlements. Racism caused our nation's only major conflict fought between our citizens on our soil, resulting in more than 600,000 casualties. The persistence of racism provoked the civil rights movement of the 1960s. The civil rights movement used the force of law and nonviolent protest to dismantle much of racism's legal vestiges. We have made considerable progress toward racial justice and equality since then, but we are yet far from the promised land. As Barb Daniels is well aware, sustained patterns of segregation in housing, persistent income gaps between blacks and whites, the continued disproportionately low numbers of minority persons in executive leadership positions in the workplace, and new waves of racial hate crimes witness to racism in our nation.

We see the nation's saga of exclusion and discrimination played out with respect to women. Enfranchised only in 1920, women have seen their numbers dramatically expand in the workforce, especially within the past few decades. With the women's movement of the 1970s, many women and men became aware of the reality of sexism for the first time. I understand sexism both as an attitude and belief and as an institutionalized pattern of social power. The attitude or belief asserts the superiority of men over women (or women over men). The institutional dimension involves the extent to which social institutions and practices use power in ways that benefit men more than women, even keeping women subordinate to men. Such institutions and practices can include marriage, laws, work organizations, the media, and violence against women. Not even the church is exempt from the painful realities of sexism. Jane Corey knows firsthand that sexist attitudes and practices are alive and well not only in the larger society but also in the church.

Feminism, which advocates the full humanity of women (and men) and which uncovers the ways in which our patriarchal society has used power to benefit men more than women, developed as a field of study and as an approach to social problems. We have made considerable social progress in combating the vestiges of sexism, but it persists as an ethical problem and challenge within society and the workplace. We see it at work in sexual harassment, in the wage gap between men and women, in the disproportionately low numbers of women in executive leadership positions within organizations, and in the differences between men's and women's experiences and perceptions of their work and their work organizations. Many more women than men experience their workplaces as hostile environments, and women continue to struggle as outsiders in a predominantly male-constructed world of power, rules, and institutions. At stake are not only questions of justice, equality, and fairness in the workplace. At stake more fundamentally are difficult and ambiguous questions regarding men's and women's proper roles in society.

We see exclusion and discrimination played out with respect to sexual orientation as well. Homophobia, the irrational fear and hatred of gays and lesbians, has shown its face through discrimination in the workplace. But there are deeper, more fundamental questions at stake in this issue as

Christians and others wrestle with the morality of sexual practice and sexual orientation. Americans—including Christians—are deeply divided about whether they think nonheterosexual orientations and lifestyles are morally acceptable or not. Perhaps discrimination against gays and lesbians in the workplace will never be fully overcome until U.S. society reaches a greater consensus about the moral status of nonheterosexual orientations. More realistic in the short-term, though, is the goal of eliminating overt expressions and patterns of discrimination against gays and lesbians in the workplace, based on the conviction that sexual orientation in almost all cases is irrelevant to job performance. Even if we think homosexuality is wrong, we ought not to use that as a weapon for unfair treatment in the workplace.

How can we respond to various forms of exclusion and discrimination in society and in the workplace? Some argue that they are all expressions of the historical fact that white heterosexual men have been the most powerful group in our society. Racism, sexism, and heterosexism have helped this group retain its predominant position of power. This interpretation is not meant to sound narrowly conspiratorial. It merely reflects the reality that groups other than white heterosexual men are gaining more participation and power in society and in the workplace, in part as a result of struggle and conflict. Women and minority persons continue to break some barriers in the workplace. Yet wage gaps are still high; the glass ceiling still exists.

Some have characterized the problem of eliminating discrimination as the challenge of helping white heterosexual men become more tolerant of other ways of being, knowing, and doing. The challenge, in part, is to reduce efforts to mold women, minority persons, and gays and lesbians to become more like white heterosexual men when they assume positions of institutional authority and power. Decreasing levels of discrimination and exclusion can go hand in hand with increasing our affirmation of diversity. The more we can affirm diversity as a positive social value, the less we need to set ourselves apart from others through discriminatory practices and attitudes. The less we need to make others conform to a single mold of attitudes and patterns of behavior, the more we seek the socially enriching benefits of diversity.

Valuing diversity is one effective way of diminishing discrimination within a work organization. It is a call to embrace differences with creativity and hope, in part so that human relations, productivity, teamwork, organizational effectiveness, organizational mission, and, yes, financial performance can be enhanced in the process. Expanding the role of creative dissent, enlarging managerial and operational styles of interaction, expanding the creative scope within which ideas are generated, developed, and executed—all can enhance diversity within work organizations. Organizations will likely need these commitments anyway to be successful in an integrated, global economy.

Dealing with workplace diversity will become increasingly necessary given demographic trends in U.S. society. The vast majority of new entrants into the U.S. workforce are women, members of minorities, or foreign-born persons. As this trend continues, the extent to which white men have defined, controlled, and managed most social institutions will be not only less desirable but also more difficult.

Christians have a rich theological and ethical language with which to renounce discrimination and affirm diversity. All humans share a basic equality in relation to God, as created by God, as sinners before God, as destined to serve human and nature's well-being, as called to seek just communities. God's creation is inherently diverse. The quest for inordinate conformity among people can become detrimental to personal growth and development and to the flourishing and growth of organizations and communities.

Furthermore, the universalism of Christian faith, which affirms the equality of all people created by God, acts as a challenge and corrective to all exclusionary and discriminatory practices. Social attitudes, rules, norms, and patterns that exclude individuals based on sex and gender, race, and sexual orientation are usually inappropriate and unfair (and in the workplace tend to generate less effectiveness and productivity).

As the United States moves into the global economy of the next century, we will need to develop and evolve new strategies for fostering, managing, and nurturing a more diverse workforce. Over time, this development will require attitudinal changes among new generations of workers as well as changes in the ways that power is used and distributed within organizations.

THE ROLE OF GOVERNMENT IN ECONOMIC LIFE

U.S. Christians span the political spectrum of positions concerning the proper role of government in society and in the economy. Some view the twentieth century as a series of grand experiments to define and expand the role of government in society. Most Marxist and other nondemocratic forms of government took a strongly interventionist role, not only in the restriction of political freedoms and human rights, but also in the direct, centralized control of economic institutions and decision making. Even within democratic regimes with market-oriented economies, the role of government has become more interventionist in business and social life.

In the United States, where government plays a less-pronounced role than in most Western European countries, we have seen a steady expansion of governmental responsibilities and functions throughout the century. Our federal government's regulatory functions in regard to business are firmly established in Article One of the U.S. Constitution. The late nineteenth and early twentieth centuries saw a substantial increase in government regulatory involvements as our society attempted to respond to dramatic changes resulting from industrialization. During the progressive movement, we saw the establishment of the Interstate Commerce Commission, the Sherman Antitrust Act, and the Food and Drug Act, all intended to curb and prevent business abuses and social harms. Regulatory functions continued to expand dramatically in the twentieth century. The most activist expansions of governmental activity came within the New Deal period of the thirties and the Great Society period of the sixties. More recently, we established such regulatory agencies as the Equal Employment Opportunity Commission, the Environmental Protection Agency, and the Occupational Safety and Health Administration.

The question has long since ceased to be whether or not government should regulate the economy; rather, the question is how and to what extent it should. In this sense, markets and businesses are never totally free of restraint. They are restrained by laws and regulations and by other norms and expectations that increasingly limit permissible action. At the same time, though, government regulation can enable economic freedom. The legal establishment and protection of the modern limited liability corporation have generated levels of economic activity and social prosperity that would have otherwise been impossible.

Within any Christian congregation, we will likely find members with a wide and even polarized range of convictions about the role of government in society. We will find strong liberals such as Jane Corey, who are suspicious about the market's capacity to generate socially desirable outcomes. And we will find staunch conservatives such as George Bremer, who are equally suspicious of government's capacity to create programs to generate social well-being.

Despite differences in political ethics, all our mainline Christian traditions and denominations affirm the essential moral role of government to establish and protect social order and to strive to be a guarantor of social justice for all citizens. At the same time, we can differ in our assessments of what government does well and poorly and what its proper function should be. Some have deep faith in its capacity to address and solve social problems such as poverty and to meet human needs. Others have deep distrust of its capabilities. Questions about the welfare state come to the surface quickly, for the welfare functions of government, especially in a federal system such as the United States, shape the ways that government becomes involved in business and economic life.

Taxation of business becomes an issue of fairness and economic justice. What are fair and appropriate taxes for business in relation to taxes for individuals? And for small businesses in relation to large businesses? How will changes in tax burdens affect some differently from others, and what are the projected consequences of the changes? What are the trade-offs, and do we find them acceptable? Do we consider the shifts in tax burden fair or unfair? Are various subsidies and tax credits granted to some businesses and industries fair?

The additional social requirements of business also become ethically relevant. Currently, our nation is debating this issue in relation to health care. Specifically, how will we involve employers in providing universal health care benefits for workers? How will private and public sectors be involved in the provision, management, and cost containment of health care?

Regulation of business is an issue of fairness and justice. At stake are the role and scope of freedom and enterprise, values that will be more important within a more dynamic global economy. At stake will be the ways and extent to which we use laws to pursue and promote diversity within an organization's workforce. At stake will be the combination of incentives and disincentives that governments provide for various kinds of employment, capital, and debt. At stake will be the environmental impacts that we deem acceptable. At stake is the division of responsibilities that we allocate to government and to business as our society tries to respond to social problems such as workforce reductions. For instance, what kinds of social safety nets should government provide to displaced workers, and what kinds of measures should be left in the hands of employers? And at a more basic level, what kinds of government social policies might be most effective in minimizing worker obsolescence (for example, the creation of stronger and more effective educational systems that give our citizens the skills and abilities to keep them competitively employed in the global economy)?

As we move more rapidly toward an integrated global economy, we raise questions about the regulation of business across nation-states. Are nation-states sufficiently powerful to regulate businesses whose activities extend beyond any single nation-state? Or has the rough balance of power and countervailing power between businesses, governments, and other sources of social power shifted in favor of global corporations? Will we need to rely increasingly on regulatory institutions that stand above nation-states, such as the United Nations, GATT, regional forms of collaboration such as NAFTA, and international treaties and protocols such as the Montreal Protocol? Strong growing evidence suggests the latter. It is likely that no single nation-state, even the United States, will have sufficient economic power to dictate a framework of regulations as was possible in the past. Political power is likely to shift away from older sources of economic power to become more evenly dispersed around the globe. At the end of World War II, the United States produced 50 percent of the world's industrial wealth. We now produce approximately 25 percent. That percentage will likely continue to drop even though our GDP will continue to grow.

THE NATURAL ENVIRONMENT: SUSTAINING PLANET EARTH

Lurking above, beneath, and beyond all other ethical issues within economic life stands a challenge far more profound and complex—the health and well-being of nature and our planet itself. Judgments can be complicated enough when we restrict our thinking only to human well-being. But when we also factor into them the effects of our actions on the myriad of mutually interdependent species and ecosystems on our planet, morality has reached utmost complexity. In this sense, environmental issues are fundamentally religious and ethical. They comprise the totality of life on earth. At issue is the relationship of humans to the rest of nature. At stake are the health and well-being of millions of species, ecosystems, and the totality of life itself as we know it, including our species. Such matters beg for theological understanding and meaning. They demand that we, as Christians, ask ourselves who we are as creatures on this fragile earth, how we should value the rest of nature, and how we must redefine our proper stewardship role in the face of ecological challenges that may threaten the very survival of our planet.

This predicament is largely our doing. Throughout history, we have progressed in our capacity to radically change our natural habitats for the benefit of human life and society. The agricultural revolution permitted increases in human population. The industrial revolution, with its rapidly expanding technologies, has had the most dramatic effects on the earth and us. Engineering constructed ever more sophisticated edifices and mechanical devices for human use. Engineering also discovered how to use the heat and energy generated from fossil fuels (coal, oil, natural gas) for human advantage. Medicine effectively fought diseases that had constrained human population growth. These advances have been most profoundly felt within economic life, which lies at the heart of most technological innovation and change. The world's human population has exploded from one billion to over five billion in this century alone. Standards of living have risen dramatically, even exponentially, for large portions of the world's population. Yet not all people have an improved quality of life. Nearly one billion people are malnourished and/or lack other minimal life necessities.

The rapid growth of human population and standards of living has come at a cost to nature, and perhaps at a substantial long-term cost to future human generations as well. Exploding human populations inevitably disrupt ecosystems and the interconnected equilibria of species. Species are becoming extinct at rates far in excess of what is typical of the natural evolutionary process. And we are uncertain about the consequences of these high rates of extinction. Wilderness, forest, and prairie are converted for agricultural use. Farmland is converted to residential, industrial, and commercial use. Human expansion almost inevitably means disruption and reduction of biodiversity. Pollution by-products of human activity leave their harmful effects on air, water, and land. Technological breakthroughs that permitted us to burn coal, oil, and natural gas for human benefit—to heat our homes and offices, to run our automobiles, and to power our industrial enterprises—have resulted in high consumption patterns in which we are using these fossil fuels at rates far in excess of the earth's natural capacities to replenish them.

We seem to be the victims of our success at manipulating nature for our benefit. For this success comes at the expense of other species and often at the expense of healthy ecosystems, some of which we may be irreparably harming. It may also come at the expense of future human generations if we do severe and irreparable damage to the earth's fundamental capacity to sustain life itself as we know it. If human population growth continues at high rates, if pollution by-products continue to accumulate, especially in less-developed countries, and if nonrenewable energy sources continue to diminish, generating future energy shocks, we, and the earth, could suffer increasingly severe harm.

Environmental problems, once predominantly local, such as a toxic waste spill, are becoming global. The release of chlorofluorocarbons (CFCs) into the stratosphere threatens to produce damaging holes in the ozone layer. Unfortunately, our scientific knowledge about the extent of damage and probable trends with respect to CFCs and ozone is yet limited. Although we live with uncertainty, we have taken decisive steps, through the Montreal Protocol, to try to solve the ozone problem by agreeing to cease production of CFCs by the end of the decade. The increase in carbon emissions from fossil fuels, notably for heating and transportation, may contribute to global warming, which could result in harmful climate changes around the globe. Scientific data are still too inconclusive for us to generate reliable conclusions; however, some governments are trying to halt increases in CO_2 emissions.

Yet our global consumption of fossil fuels increases annually, hastening the day when more severe scarcities will prohibit current widespread use, forcing even greater efficiencies and the search for alternative energy sources. If we are unprepared for the inevitable transition to renewable sources of energy, future generations may suffer severe shocks, including reductions in population and in standards of living. Global population growth rates are modest in most of the developed world and are beginning to come down in many parts of the less-developed world, but actual growth in population continues to be high. Today's global population of more than five billion is projected to double sometime during the next century. Even with improved efficiencies in energy use, global energy consumption will continue to expand in the foreseeable future as will human demands on other resources.

At some point we may compromise the carrying capacity of the earth to sustain life in healthy ecosystems. Humanity will have acquired new levels of power and dominance; we may one day have the capacity radically to degrade the earth's sustainability, not through nuclear warfare, but through normal human activities.

Our ultimate ecological destiny may be certain. Our shorter-term destiny is not. Our choices, actions, and policies *can* affect the quality of human lives and societies, and the health of ecosystems and the earth as a whole. And it is here that our faith, with its rich reserve of ethical resources, can empower us to think, act, and live responsibly within God's fragile world. If God created humans and all other creatures on earth, do not these creatures have value and worth not merely for their usefulness to us but also intrinsically as created by God? Does not God's creation require from us an attitude of deep reverence and awe? Would not such reverence and awe suggest a strong ethic of care for the earth? Reflect on the theological and ethical resources of chapter 3, and consider the relevance of concepts like stewardship and the common good, understood not only as the good of humans but also of the well-being of God's larger ecological community of life. If such a larger common good became our ethical aim, then our understanding of what has value and our sense of ethical obligation would become greatly expanded (and much more complicated). These resources of our faith can shape our vision and understanding of environmental problems and can help us make choices in our everyday lives regarding how we will live on planet earth.

These daily choices constitute the "more or less" of our ethical existence.

We learn from our mistakes and sometimes correct some harms to society and to nature. We have made great strides in improving air quality in the United States, largely due to changes mandated by the 1970 Clear Air Act and now strengthened by the 1990 Clean Air Act. Efforts at energy conservation can make a difference. Technological advances produce ever more efficient means to use energy. Throughout the century, transportation vehicles have become more fuel efficient. We continue to find more efficient ways to insulate, heat, and cool buildings. Production processes become ever more energy efficient. We search for ways to reduce our dependence on nonrenewable fossil fuels, especially oil. Natural gas, cleaner than oil and coal, may be more widely used in the next several decades. More commercial vehicle fleets are being converted to natural gas. Beyond such a transitional period, we will need to convert to renewable sources of energy such as wind, hydrogen, and the sun if we are to sustain high levels of population, economic development, and energy consumption.

In addition to energy conservation and transition, we need to find more ways to reduce pollution by-products of energy consumption. Emission standards for transportation vehicles and industry continue to be strengthened, resulting in substantial reductions in harmful sulfur and carbon emissions. Within the United States, we have dramatically reduced the exhaust emissions of passenger cars. According to the Environmental Protection Agency, by 1992, auto emissions of hydrocarbons had been reduced 96 percent, carbon monoxide 96 percent, and nitrogen oxides 76 percent from their 1960 levels. Smog does not cloud the Los Angeles skyline like it did twenty years ago. Technology will be a vital part of the solution as we develop cleaner technologies to satisfy human needs. But as Christians, we must recognize the issue as more than technological. It goes to the heart of who we are and how we value and use nature.

Will such advances in our nation be sufficient and timely enough to offset other global trends, most notably in the less-developed world? Although per capita energy consumption in many less-developed world countries is only about 10 percent of that in the United States, dramatic increases in population and economic development will increase the less-developed world's total share of global energy consumption over time. Paradoxically, the moral imperative of global economic development will mean increased demands on scarce sources of energy. Most less-developed countries are unable to devote adequate amounts of national spending for environmental protection, such as the development of clean water supplies, adequate sanitation systems, and vehicle emissions controls.

Some development economists argue that economic development will generate more environmentally friendly and sustainable agricultural, industrial, and energy use patterns. Only as countries develop high-enough levels of national disposable income can they devote more financial resources to environmental protection and regulation. Economic development may be an essential ingredient to a more environmentally sustainable future. Population birthrates historically come down when standards of living increase. Whether the numerical increases in population will peak and reverse themselves before we irreparably compromise the earth's carrying capacity, though, is an important open question upon which depends the future of our planet.

These environmental challenges are converging to create a new environmental consciousness within industrialized countries and elsewhere around the globe. We are learning how to respond more effectively. Some environmental problems require cross-sectoral and multinational collaboration, made clear by the signing of the Montreal Protocol. In that

protocol, virtually all nations agreed to terminate the production and distribution of CFCs by the end of the decade.
The process received strong support and leadership from
the DuPont Corporation, the world's leading producer of
CFCs. Not only are corporations now seeking and developing cost-effective substitutes for CFCs that are less destructive to the environment, but funds are mandated to assist
less-developed countries in their technological conversion to
non-CFCs as well. We are responding to a problem of global
dimensions with a solution of global dimensions.

Governments and businesses seek ways more fully to factor into the price of a good or service its full cost to users and
the environment, both beneficial and harmful. Consumers'
choices will thus become more environmentally sensitive.
Business will change more readily when incentive structures
more clearly encourage environmentally friendly practices.
Consumers will change habits as well when prices more fully
reflect environmental impacts.

As noted in chapter 3, the natural environment has only
recently become a topic of deliberation for Christian theology and ethics. Historically, nature was virtually ignored as a
subject of moral relevance. We deemed it of little or no moral
value because we thought it was an inert and endless supply
of resources, or we considered its moral relevance only for
its instrumental value to serve human material needs. Those
views were supported by our tendency to interpret scripture,
notably the creation story in Genesis and our mandate to be
stewards of nature, in terms of our domination over nature
and its subordination to our will.

We are now faced with the challenge to rethink our
theological understanding of nature and our interpretation
of biblical texts more in terms of human participation and
cooperation with nature. We do this in light of new evidence,
which has demonstrated the fragility and finitude of nature
when confronted with ever more taxing patterns of human

life. And we are faced with the challenge to act and live in ways that show respect and care for God's creation. And as individual Christians who are consumers and workers, we will be challenged to find ways to modify our use of the earth's resources and live within its fragile ecosystems.

QUESTIONS FOR GROUP STUDY AND DISCUSSION

1. Have you or others you know experienced a layoff or termination in employment due to a plant closing or workforce reduction? Has your work organization?

2. How have you or those you know coped with this situation?

3. What do you think are the larger causes of this trend?

4. How do you respond as a Christian? What ethical resources of faith can you employ to understand and respond to this challenging trend?

5. What are the responsibilities of workers, businesses, unions, governments, churches, and other social institutions?

6. Have you experienced discrimination or exclusion in the workplace?

7. To what extent do you believe forms of discrimination based on race, sex, or sexual orientation still exist?

8. How do your race, gender, and sexual orientation affect the way you view the reality of discrimination?

9. How should society best respond to discrimination? How should work organizations best respond?

10. What creative and strategic opportunities do you have as a worker to combat discrimination and affirm diversity and multiculturalism?

11. How do you assess the role of government in society and in relation to business?

12. What ethical issues do you find most important and deeply embedded within government's social roles?

13. How will government regulation of business need to change in a global economy?

14. What do you think are the most important environmental issues facing our country and the global society?

15. How have environmental issues affected your life as a consumer and your lifestyle choices and patterns?

16. How have environmental issues affected your workplace and the policies, practices, and behavior of your work organization?

17. What do you think are effective strategies for our society to respond to environmental challenges and problems?

18. How should we attempt to employ the resources of Christian faith to understand and respond to environmental challenges?

KEY RESOURCES

Brown, Lester, ed. *State of the World*. New York: Norton. Produced by the Worldwatch Institute, this is an annual volume. The reader is encouraged to obtain any recent edition.

Clegg, Stewart R. *Modern Organizations: Organization Studies in the Postmodern World.* London: Sage, 1990.

Daly, Herman, ed. *Economics, Ecology, Ethics: Essays Toward a Steady-State Economy.* San Francisco: W. H. Freeman and Co., 1980.

Ethical Considerations in Corporate Takeovers. Washington, D.C.: Woodstock Theological Center. Georgetown University Press, 1990.

Gore, Al. *Earth in the Balance: Ecology and the Human Spirit.* Boston: Houghton Mifflin, 1992.

Gustafson, James. *The Natural Environment from a Theocentric Perspective.* Cleveland: Pilgrim, 1994.

Haughey, John. "The Growing Dilemma of Loyalty and the Firm." In Samuel M. Natala and Brian M. Rothschild, eds., *Work Values: Education, Organization, and Religious Concerns.* The Netherlands, Rodopi Publishers, 1994, pp. 183-96.

Jackson, Susan E. *Diversity in the Workplace: Human Resources Initiatives.* New York: Guilford, 1992.

Jamieson, David, and Julie O'Mara. *Managing Workforce 2000: Gaining the Diversity Advantage.* San Francisco: Jossey-Bass, 1991.

Johnson, William B. *Workforce 2000: Work and Workers for the 21st Century.* Indianapolis: Hudson Institute, 1987.

Morrison, Ann M., et al. *Breaking the Glass Ceiling: Can Women Reach the Top of America's Largest Corporations?* Redding, Mass.: Addison-Wesley, 1989.

Nash, James A. *Loving Nature: Ecological Integrity and Christian Responsibility.* Nashville: Abingdon Press, 1991.

Pfarr, Suzanne. *Homophobia: A Weapon of Sexism.* Inverness, Calif.: Chardon, 1988.

Santmire, H. Paul. *The Travail of Nature: The Ambiguous Ecological Promise of Christian Theology.* Philadelphia: Fortress, 1985.

World Bank Staff. *World Development Report 1992: Development and the Environment.* New York: Oxford University Press, 1992.

CHAPTER SIX

Strategies for Congregations

I F WE ARE TO KEEP our faith at work, we do well to seek ways that our congregations can aid us in this vital task. We must identify ways in which our participation in the community of faith can nurture us and provide us with resources that strengthen our efforts as faithful Christians in the workplace. Churches have always been places where moral formation and reflection take place. Yet work and economic life are seldom adequately addressed within the congregation.

In this chapter, we address the practical challenge of making work and economic concerns a more important dimension of the life and practice of congregations. We consider some reasons for the neglect or lack of emphasis on workplace and economic issues. I try to identify some stumbling blocks to overcome so that connections between faith and work can become more vital and moral reflection can be developed and strengthened in this area. I propose a vision of the church as a community of moral deliberation and mutual learning, and I outline strategies, practical guidelines, and programmatic suggestions for nurturing such activity within the congregation.

Churches are not all alike. We differ in our understandings of what it means to be a member of a church and what it means to be the church. Our various traditions and denominations differ widely on a range of issues such as the role and authority of Scripture and theological tradition, the role and authority of ordination and church leadership, types of church structure and polity, the role of the local congregation, sacraments, and the means of grace. Churches also differ in their positions on capitalism and economic life, as evidenced in church social statements and pronouncements. Episcopal models, such as Roman Catholicism, differ from congregational polities, such as Baptist and the United Church of Christ (UCC). Each responds differently when asked, "Who speaks for the church?" and "Where does authority lie?" The pope, bishops, synods of bishops, churches in convention or assembly, local congregations, individual believers, ecumenical associations such as the World Council of Churches—each of these expressions of the church has something to say about the relationship of Christian faith to work and economic life. For our purposes in this book, we will focus on one dimension of the church—the local congregation.

I offer proposals for enhancing connections between faith and work that might be considered and implemented within any congregation, regardless of its tradition or denomination. I assume that work and economic life should be morally relevant topics for any church and that Christian ethical reflection about such matters is strongly implied, if not mandated, within any Christian faith tradition. We may disagree about what precisely it means to be a Christian in the world. We may have different ways of thinking about the issues. We will sometimes arrive at different, even conflicting, moral conclusions and prescriptions. But *all* Christians and faith traditions share the responsibility to wrestle with such concerns.

Congregations of every stripe can become communities of moral deliberation and mutual learning in which members are challenged, provoked, supported, enlivened, and inspired to make connections between their faith and their work. And they can empower members to be effective Christians in the workplace and in economic life. For all their differences, George Bremer, Byron Newcomb, Barb Daniels, Jane Corey, and Mark O'Grady wish their congregations to be places where faith nurtures and inspires members at work.

STUMBLING BLOCKS TO EFFECTIVE MINISTRY

The need for such ministry and discernment in our churches is enormous. Yet barriers and obstacles within many congregations prevent such discussion and discernment from occurring. Let's take a quick look at them before we consider how to move ahead. Though it does not provide any detailed rebuttals or responses to these obstacles, this book is a source of insights, concepts, and resources for your congregation to overcome these very problems and for you to make more effective connections between your faith and your work. Take a few moments to consider how you might respond to each of these problems if they exist for you or for your congregation.

1. *Many Christians do not think about their faith as having any important connection to work and economic life.* Some connect faith primarily to more intimate spheres of life and to specifically church-related activities. For many, church involvement revolves primarily around personal life and relationships, such as family. Religion is a support for this institution and for personal nurture and well-being. Many do not look to religion for guidance about work and economic life. For some, this separation or lack of connection may be driven by the assumption that religion and faith have nothing to say about economic life. Some believe that economic life is autonomous—it is driven by norms or laws completely independent of religion and Christian ethics. The Christian, or anyone else, must identify and understand these autonomous norms and live by them within their

sphere. In other words, Christian faith and ethics have no place at work and in economic life. The sacred and the secular are separate.

Yet such a position denies the sovereignty of God over all spheres of life. It also ignores the rich discussions of economic life found throughout Scripture, such as in the Hebrew Scriptures and in the teachings of Jesus. (It also ignores the tradition of natural law found within some Roman Catholic theology that asserts the universal capacity of human reason to discern the good from the orderings of human life and experience.)

2. *Economic life is so complex that it is difficult to understand and to address within one's religious life and community of faith.* This understanding can sometimes result from a personal feeling of powerlessness or even resignation and despair about economic matters—they seem so large and unchangeable that we don't feel we know how to make any real impact on economic life. And when debate about complex issues generates moral difference and disagreement within a congregation, we may be reluctant to deal with such disagreement. Such experiences can be divisive to relationships, something that some find threatening to the spirit of nurture, care, and mutual support that many desire from their congregation. Learning how to deal with complexity and moral difference becomes essential to greater effectiveness in this area for the community of faith.

3. *Many Christians feel illiterate and/or lacking in confidence in their theological understandings of faith and in their comfort levels to speak with others about their faith.* Even though we may be lifelong Christians and long-standing members of a particular denomination or church, profoundly simple questions such as "What does your Christian faith mean to you?" or "How does your Christian faith inform and guide your life?" can sometimes take us by surprise and perplex us, and result in answers that we feel are inadequate. Many of us feel

only remotely familiar with Scripture and feel we know little about the theological traditions of our denominations. Some feel unpracticed in the art of Christian ethical judgment.

4. *Many clergy feel that they lack basic expertise in economic and workplace concerns and therefore do not emphasize such connections within their ministerial roles and leadership capacities within their congregations.* Most congregations already place countless expectations on their clergy—leading worship, teaching Scripture, providing pastoral care, and handling administrative duties involved with congregational leadership. Many clergy are stretched so thin that they feel overwhelmed at the thought of trying to expand their professional expertise and programmatic efforts into another area.

5. *Within some congregations, members may feel that their clergy and/or denominations, through preaching or official pronouncements, hold viewpoints and draw conclusions that are far different from their own, making discussion and deliberation difficult or uncomfortable.* On many social ethical topics, clergy and official denominational positions tend to express moral judgments perceived as more progressive, liberal, left wing, or change oriented than those of the people in the pew. Sometimes, this divergence of positions leads to members' attitudes of disregard or even hostility. I suspect that few laypersons could not find some official denominational position with which they disagree or dissent strongly. To acknowledge such divergence is not necessarily to suggest that one position is morally superior to the other. It is merely to point out what can become a stumbling block within a congregation (as well as an opportunity for growth and learning).

These, and other, stumbling blocks may exist within your church. They need not be insurmountable obstacles, though. Let's consider some positive steps, activities, and strategies that congregations might take to overcome these obstacles and create stronger ministry in this area. The aim is to create and nurture communities of moral deliberation and mutual learning where members are supported, informed, and inspired to live faithfully in their work and in economic life.

ENLIVENING THE CONNECTIONS WITHIN CONGREGATIONS

Let's look at these key components of congregational life: worship, pastoral care, social ministry, and education.

Worship. In most congregations, worship is the most important activity. Although this is certainly true of a sacramental tradition such as Anglicanism, which grounds its theology and ethics in worship, it is true for churches from other traditions and denominations as well. What single activity within the life of a congregation draws the most participants and most defines its identity? Whatever else members may do within their congregations, they are most likely to attend worship. Worship becomes the single most decisive way that congregations of all stripes inform and shape their members' experiences of faith and of God. If there is any prominent way that congregations communicate the message and meaning of Christian faith among their members, it is through worship. To cite Timothy Sedgwick:

> Worship relates faith and life. In worship the story of Christian faith is told, including both an understanding of God and God's purposes and of the life in response to God. But worship does more than express the meaning of Christian faith. . . . In worship the participant is changed and formed in relation to God. To begin with worship and the worshipping community is to begin at the center of Christian faith in the experience of conversion and reconciliation. (*Sacramental Ethics*, pp. 14-15)

To worship, then, we must turn in our quest for valuable and creative resources for linking faith and work and for shaping a Christian ethic at work.

For congregations from most faith traditions, liturgy is the focus of worship. The English word *liturgy* comes from the Greek word *leitourgia,* which combines the word for "public" *(leitos)* with the word for "work" *(ergon),* which translates literally as "work of the people." In the New Testament, *leitourgia* referred to services in the temple as well as to the ongoing life of the Christian community.

Since worship is so important to the formation of Christians and to our identity as a community of faith, we need to mine its resources for shaping a Christian ethic for work. Let me propose two ways. First, we can examine more closely the standard liturgical components of worship used within a denomination and congregation to consider their implications for our work. Second, we can insert occasional rituals and activities into worship celebrating the creative ways that individual members live out their faith within the workplace or that make a statement about how the community of faith sees itself in relation to economic life.

First, let us consider the standard liturgical components of our worship services. Let me illustrate briefly with some examples from Lutheran and Methodist worship. In the *Lutheran Book of Worship (LBW)* used by the Evangelical Lutheran Church in America, we find the following words of confession at the beginning of the liturgy, spoken by the congregation:

> We confess that we are in bondage to sin and cannot free ourselves. We have sinned against you in thought, word, and deed, by what we have done and by what we have left undone. We have not loved you with our whole heart; we have not loved our neighbor as ourselves. For the sake of your Son, Jesus Christ, have mercy on us. Forgive us, renew us, and lead

us, so that we may delight in your will and walk in your ways,
to the glory of your holy name. Amen.

This confession of sin encompasses all aspects of life,
including work. It views humans not as utterly depraved and
evil but as corrupted good. What good we do is insufficient
to satisfy God's moral requirements. We seek not only God's
mercy and forgiveness but also God's power to change and
transform us as moral agents in the world. We seek God's
renewal and guidance so that we might be empowered better
to do the good that God wills. As Christians, we are challenged to consider the meaning of this confession of sin and
request for moral renewal and guidance within situations at
work.

Also in the *LBW* are the following prayers of Setting One
of the liturgy for Holy Communion (to be recited by the
congregation after the offering and prior to the Great
Thanksgiving):

We offer with joy and thanksgiving what you have first given
us—our selves, our time, and our possessions, signs of your
gracious love. Receive them for the sake of him who offered
himself for us, Jesus Christ our Lord. Amen.

[or]

O Lord our God, maker of all things. Through your goodness
you have blessed us with these gifts. With them we offer
ourselves to your service and dedicate our lives to the care
and redemption of all that you have made, for the sake of
him who gave himself for us, Jesus Christ our Lord. Amen.

In these prayers, the Christian life is viewed as a gift from
God. Everything we have is a sign of God's gracious love for
us. These gifts include our efforts at work, including the skills
and abilities we use there, and our possessions—the tangible

results of our work and of economic life itself. God has created the conditions that make work and economic life possible. Our work efforts and their results become gifts that we are called to give back to God. Hence, our work itself is viewed as an offering to God, symbolized within the liturgy in the receiving of offerings and in the community's placement of these sacrificial gifts on God's altar. This act further symbolizes our intent to recommit and rededicate our lives to the service, care, and redemption of all of God's creation. We reaffirm that all spheres of life, including work, fall within the embrace of God's sovereignty and moral demands. This liturgy weaves together prominent theological themes—sin, grace, sovereignty, stewardship, and care for creation.

In the worship service of The United Methodist Church (*The United Methodist Hymnal,* A Service of Word and Table I), we find these words from the Great Thanksgiving, immediately before the administration of Communion:

> And so, in remembrance of these your mighty acts in Jesus Christ, we offer ourselves in praise and thanksgiving as a holy and living sacrifice, in union with Christ's offering for us, as we proclaim the mystery of faith.

Again the Christian life is characterized as one of praise and thanksgiving, offered to God as a result of faith. Our work and economic activities are viewed as a living sacrifice to God.

Whatever your denomination, you will likely find elements from the standard liturgical rites and practices used in your congregation that reveal and illuminate connections between faith and work. Hymns and choral music also make theological and ethical connections. Our various traditions of sacred music are replete with hymns and other songs that include themes of work, vocation, stewardship, and Christian witness in society. Examples include "Called to God's Mission," "Lord of All Hopefulness" (Slane), and "Forth in Thy Name, O Lord, I Go." Special petitions within prayers of the people can directly address workplace issues and concerns. And through sermons and homilies, preachers can do theological and ethical reflection on contemporary economic life and on the work realities faced by members of the congregation.

A recent comprehensive study of Roman Catholic, Protestant (mainline and evangelical), and Jewish congregations in the Chicago area conducted by the Center for Ethics and Corporate Policy found that work is one of the least likely topics to be addressed in sermons. However, most members of these congregations not only desired their clergy to devote *more* attention to work and economic life in their sermons, but also claimed that they gained more satisfaction from their congregations to the extent that work issues were more frequently and directly addressed in sermons.

A second way that worship can be a more vital resource for connecting faith and work is to create occasional special rituals and activities to include within the worship service. Special rituals can call attention to and celebrate the creative ways that members live out their faith in the workplace. As we sometimes commission individuals when they assume special roles in the congregation (e.g., officers, trustees, educators), so might we symbolically commission members to serve society in their occupational roles. For instance, *The United Methodist Book of Worship (UMBW)* is filled with examples of special prayers that can be offered for specific individuals experiencing important transitions related to their work lives, such as the beginning of a new job (#538) or of retirement (#543), as well as general petitions for those who work (#539, #540) and for those who are unemployed (#541). This petition can be offered for an individual starting a new job:

> Lord Jesus Christ, carpenter of creation,
>> you knew the satisfactions and responsibilities of human work and hallowed it for ever in a carpenter's shop in Nazareth.

As *[person's name]* begins a new job,
> as a worthy occupation, may it be useful in the human
> enterprise.

May *[person's name]* be a blessing to others
> by living and working to the honor and glory of your holy
> name. Amen. (#538)

In addition, special festivals and Sundays in the liturgical year as well as national holidays provide opportunities to integrate the theme of work into worship, such as Reformation Sunday, Labor Day, Student Day, Laity Sunday (again see, for instance, *UMBW* for helpful suggestions).

Or as a part of the receiving of offerings, what if we were to ritualistically bring forward to the altar and offer to God some of the standard tools and accoutrements of work to symbolize the theological and moral meanings of our occupational roles? Can you imagine placing hammers and wrenches, brooms and cleaning materials, law manuals and Internal Revenue Service tax codes, PCs and floppy disks, and briefcases and cellular phones on the altar in the front of your church? Wouldn't that have a startling impact on the minds of many members? We cannot ignore or minimize the importance of the many nonverbal sensual dimensions of worship in shaping our religious and ethical identities as Christians.

Pastoral Care and Mutual Support

Another congregational resource for fostering connections between faith and work is pastoral care and mutual support among members. A primary function that most clergy play for members is pastoral care. This care can consist of counseling for individuals, family units, and small groups of members. Such counseling often revolves around crisis points in the lives of individuals (the death of a loved one, unexpected illnesses, or injuries); problems and challenges in personal relationships (love relationships, marriages, and parent-child relationships); substance abuse problems; life cycle challenges and problems such as those encountered in adolescence, midlife, and older years; questions of religious and personal meaning, identity, and self-doubt.

Pastoral care can and does occur around economic and workplace concerns, yet often much less frequently than might be desired. Individuals wrestle with their vocational identities and roles. Economic hardships can strain their sense of self-esteem. Job loss can shatter their sense of vocational self-identity, confidence, and security as well as challenge the fragile sustainability of family units. Questionable or unethical actions or patterns within one's work organization can cause emotional stress and moral ambiguity and uncertainty as to how to respond or whether to remain within the organization. In these situations, pastoral care can help individuals respond to hardships, calamities, or tragedies by identifying spiritual, ethical, and communal resources and supports to empower them to cope, understand, and creatively move forward with their lives within a religious framework of meaning.

Pastoral care can also be an empowering resource to enable individuals to understand and respond creatively to positive challenges and opportunities in the workplace. Should I accept an exciting job promotion or transfer? What do I do with more vocational power and responsibilities? How can I see my vocational time and skills, and my financial resources, as opportunities for faithful Christian witness and stewardship? For instance, Byron Newcomb, who sees his role and power as an advertiser as an opportunity to shape the world in a way consistent with his vision of faith, can benefit greatly from ongoing pastoral care and spiritual direction with his pastor. Father Mark O'Grady is grateful when his parishioners trust him enough to share their personal struggles at work, with the goal of seeking greater spiritual and ethical discernment.

Unfortunately, many clergy lament that their members often fail to use pastoral care as a means for bringing economic and workplace concerns within the purview of spiritual self-identity. In addition, far too many members, rightly or wrongly, do not wish to come to their clergypersons for pastoral care related to workplace concerns. Pastoral care, whether as a response to problems or to positive opportunities, becomes a vital congregational resource for helping members clarify their vocational self-understanding and seek moral discernment about economic and workplace issues.

Clergy might consider making work calls to their members in their workplaces as a way to do pastoral care and as a way to learn more about the work lives of their members. Imagine a clergyperson spending a full day in your workplace, observing your work, seeing your interactions with others, your decisions, dilemmas, and challenges, and then debriefing this experience together. Imagine a clergyperson doing twenty or thirty or fifty of these with other members of your congregation in vastly different work settings. Clergy would be thrown into the real-life world of their members in a way that might reshape, broaden, and deepen their sense of vocational identity. And they might gain new insights into where the congregation's ministry might most effectively be directed, based on the needs and issues that surface from such visits.

Spiritual care and moral encouragement need never be restricted to clergy-member pastoral care relationships. Members of congregations should be encouraged to see each other as ministers, able to offer nurture and support, personal care and moral reflection for each other. If a congregation is to be the Body of Christ, it ought to be a place where mutual support and nurture occur. Members, as fellow participants in the secular workplace, often can minister to each other more effectively with respect to economic and workplace issues than can clergy. Sometimes the person who can best offer care and ministry to someone tested by a work-related crisis such as an unexpected job loss is the person who has gone through it.

Some congregations have formed support groups of members who come together, usually informally, for sharing, support, nurture, and mutual discernment. Such groups might be organized according to profession or occupation (e.g., lawyers, accountants, health care professionals, human resource professionals), or they might be mixed, permitting a rich diversity of viewpoints and perspectives. They might vary in format and style, depending on the needs, comfort levels, and religious styles and traditions represented by members. For instance, the group format might include prayer, reflection on scripture, brief worship, theological reflection, or more informal conversation and discernment. In any case, members are able to share their questions, concerns, uncertainties, fears, and painful experiences about work in the light of their faith among a small community of persons in a spirit of care, trust, and mutual support and nurture. Churches might also consider appointing and training volunteers to have specialized ministries of care and support with respect to work (a specialized diaconate ministry) that are available to all members of the congregation or the wider community. Such a formalized ministry might be open-ended to meet a variety of needs, or it might be focused, for instance, to help unemployed persons cope with their situation and seek new employment.

Social Ministry

Social ministry consists of the ways a congregation and its members live out corporate and personal visions of faith in the world. Quite literally, all ministry is social, for we can never do ministry outside the fabric of social relationships. I understand social ministry as activities and programs of a congregation and its members that serve, shape, or benefit the larger world outside the walls of the worshiping, confessing community of faith. Broadly defined, then, social ministry involves all actions in which Christians engage that spring from our self-understanding of what it means to be a Christian in the world. How we participate in all spheres of life—intimate relationships, family, work, politics, civic associations, interactions with nature—can be viewed as social ministry. Social ministry includes congregational involvement in local communities. It involves denominational activities at a larger churchwide level. It involves our connections with activities and programs across the globe.

Let's look at some brief examples of how congregational social ministry can enliven the connections between faith and work. Effective social ministry in this area will strive to meet the real and felt needs of individuals as they struggle to connect their faith and their work. Some congregations have established unemployment support groups, job networking groups, and professional career development and retraining programs that help individuals cope with hardships of job loss and move through the transition to new work. Other congregations become intentionally involved in public policy debates at local, state, national, and international levels, attempting to shape governmental policies and responses to problems. Some may become involved as advocates of a particular cause, such as the new social investment movement that encourages selective capital investments in newly emergent multiracial, democratic societies abroad such as Namibia and South Africa, as well as in disadvantaged or underdeveloped areas within our country. Other congregations may wish to create or support activities that benefit disadvantaged groups such as homeless people, persons who are mentally ill, or persons from chronically low-income neighborhoods. Some middle-class North American congregations, for instance, have become sister congregations with congregations from other parts of the world, actively sponsoring collaborative ministries, forms of financial assistance, and/or cross visits.

Education

Throughout our churches, Christians are hungry for educational opportunities to probe their work lives in light of their faith. In my six years as director of a church- and corporate-sponsored ethics center in Chicago, I conducted educational programs on Christian ethics and work for members of many Roman Catholic and Protestant congregations. In most of these churches, our seminar provided the first sustained opportunity for members to talk to each other about their work and to consider the ethical challenges with which they wrestle as Christians in the workplace. In every congregation, we found thoughtful participants who wanted to make connections and probe the meaning of Christian faith and ethics for work and economic life. We found scores of individuals who had thought about these matters for years but had rarely, if ever, brought them to the table for discussion and reflection within their faith communities. Individual members usually have a multitude of questions about the ethical character of their work roles, their work organizations, and the larger economy, yet they rarely seem to do Christian moral reflection together *as members of a faith community.* To characterize this gap or deficiency in a positive light, we can say that our churches are challenged to become more effective and vital communities of moral deliberation and mutual learning.

We may know something about the work roles and identities of our fellow members (Bill Smith is an accountant at ABC Corporation; Mary Goode was just laid off at Abco, Inc.), but we seldom bring these roles explicitly into conversations within Christian education programs. Rather, we are more likely to know Mary Goode as John Goode's spouse and as Cindy and Sally Goode's mother, and Bill Smith as the stewardship committee chairman and a choir member.

Educational programs that attempt to connect faith and work and that try to foster Christian ethical reflection about work and economic life can take many forms. Let me mention several possibilities:

- *Panel discussions.* Consider organizing two or three consecutive panel discussions, each of which might feature three or four members who briefly describe their work and reflect on its meaning as Christians. Individuals can identify their ethical problems and challenges, discuss how they understand their work spiritually, and comment on how their faith does or does not support and sustain them as they seek to perform their jobs well. Personal testimonials and the sharing of life experiences can be effective ways to make the issues real for members. We learn through the stories of others.

- *Case study reflection groups.* One of my Lutheran friends tells about an ongoing group of members from his congregation who have been meeting for years and reflecting on the spiritual and ethical dimensions of their work roles and organizations. For each session, one member agrees to write up a case that describes a situation or scenario from his or her workplace involving an issue, problem, or decision with ethical dimensions. Group members come prepared to reflect on the case with the writer, offering questions, suggestions, support, and deliberation. The formal process of writing up a case for discussion is an important procedural discipline that keeps the group on track. The writer of the case leads the discussion, trying to direct the group members toward the kind of support and moral discernment that he or she thinks is needed.

- *Bible study.* Regardless of denominational differences, Scripture is a normative source of moral authority for all

Christians. Scripture provides us with the story of our lives, defining who we are fundamentally as Christians. Study groups might consider a series of sessions that examine key texts from Scripture in order to reflect and discern together their meanings and insights for contemporary work life. (Clergy can be helpful here in suggesting scriptural selections.) Genesis, the Prophets, the Holiness Code, and the sayings and parables of Jesus become prime candidates for study.

- *Denominational study materials and social statements.* Virtually every Christian faith tradition and denomination has study materials and social statements that address from a theological and ethical point of view various social issues and problems, including economic life. Invite members of your congregation to form a study group that meets for a period of time to study such documents. Expect members to have very different reactions—some positive, some negative—to such statements. Create a format so that the document can be studied in its parts and a diversity of participant reactions and responses can be heard and discussed. Clergy can be helpful dialogue partners in these discussions.

- *Intensive all-day workshops or weekend retreats.* Consider structuring an intensive educational program that might include any or all of the above formats, coupled with worship, prayer, and private time for reflection, meditation, and personal renewal. Members often lament the lack of opportunity and time for unharried personal reflection, career discernment, and spiritual growth within their work settings and communities. Congregational life can promote each undertaking.

Let me conclude with some suggestions and guidelines that can enhance the success of educational efforts in your congregation:

- *Encourage mutual listening and learning.* As with virtually any significant matter, people have rich and diverse perspectives and sometimes conflicting views not only about what it means to be Christian but also what is going on in economic life today. The subject matter can become emotionally laden and charged. No one has a corner on the truth in these matters. We must listen and learn from each other.

- *Try to get clarity on the questions being asked and probed.* Many issues of business and economic life are so complex that we sometimes feel overwhelmed by their many layers. In discussions and debates, we can often talk past others by not defining our terms and by not being as clear as possible in saying what we mean. Our understandings of the facts sometimes differ substantially. For instance, while this book was being written, the U.S. public and the U.S. Congress were engaged in a substantial debate over the merits of NAFTA. With an issue such as NAFTA, we must work hard as Christians and as U.S. citizens to try to understand what NAFTA is technically, and then try to sort out which claims being made about it by the media and by economists and politicians seem to be true. And after we have attempted to understand the debate economically, we must ask ourselves how our Christian values help us make an informed moral judgment about whether we should support NAFTA's drive toward a single unified North American free trade zone.

- *Acknowledge that the church and Christians may not always have easy or singular answers to the challenges and dilemmas of economic life.* Fortunately, churches do not make Christian membership, faith, and belief dependent on a *single* view of economic life, how it ought to be run, and what our economic roles should be. The church and Christian ethics rarely provide easy or singular answers to economic challenges and issues. Rather, these are best left as matters of communal debate and discernment and of individual moral conscience.

- *Engage in dialogue in a spirit of civility and mutuality, respecting differences of perspective and conclusion, even radical differences.* The issues are complex; diverse moral perspectives and conclusions are the reality among Christians. We must learn to learn from each other in a spirit of love, civility, humility, and mutual support. Unswerving, unyielding dogmatic assertions and conclusions about what it means to connect faith and work are rarely helpful within educational settings. This is not to suggest, though, that we ought not to speak and debate with passion and conviction about what it means to be Christian in the workplace.

- *Acknowledge and exploit the vast wealth of expertise and experience within the congregation.* Though the issues can be fraught with immense complexity and moral ambiguity, we ought not to feel immobilized in our efforts to wrestle with and explore them within our congregations. Most of us do not feel like experts in the subject matter, but each congregation has treasure in earthen vessels. Among the members of the typical congregation we will find dozens, if not hundreds, of resident experts who have spent years as Christians at work. We have literally thousands of years of experience and expertise at our fingertips waiting to be tapped for educational programs that relate faith and work. Managers, accountants, physicians, business professors, computer technicians, engineers, teachers, nurses, sales and marketing professionals, assembly workers, service workers, CEOs, entrepreneurs running small family firms, and more may be in the congregation.

- *Encourage participation and planning of members.* The most effective programs tend to involve participation and planning by members. Clergy and other religious professionals can provide leadership, direction, and focus. But the vitality of Christian education programs for adults is usually enhanced by the extent to which we can tap the creative energies and planning and administrative abilities of members themselves. Steering committees, member surveys and inventories to assess possible interest in topics and/or formats, ongoing lay leadership and administration, and formalized participant evaluations can be vital keys to success in educational efforts.

QUESTIONS FOR GROUP STUDY AND DISCUSSION

1. In what ways do the activities, practices, and programs within your congregation encourage members to consider the relationship between their faith and their work?

2. Are there stumbling blocks or particular reasons why your congregation's ministry in this area may be less effective than you would like? If so, what are they?

3. What would it take to overcome such stumbling blocks or obstacles? How would your congregation need to change to make such ministry occur more effectively?

4. What are the needs of members within your congregation with regard to connecting faith and work? How could your congregation identify these needs more clearly and effectively?

5. What are the ways that worship within your congregation discloses resources and linkages between faith and work? Consider inviting a clergy member of your congregation to present the meanings and purposes of the components of your worship service and then discuss ways in which they can help us relate our faith and ethics to work and economic life.

---

6. Has your congregation sponsored educational programs that treat ethical issues in business and economic life? If so, which have been most successful?

7. What new directions would you like to see your congregation develop as it strives to be a community of moral discourse and mutual learning?

KEY RESOURCES

Diehl, William E. *Thank God, It's Monday!* Philadelphia: Fortress, 1982.

Hart, Stephen, and David A. Krueger. *Faith and Work: Personal Response and Challenges for Congregations.* Chicago: Center for Ethics and Corporate Policy, 1991.

Haughey, John C. *Converting 9 to 5: A Spirituality of Daily Work.* New York: Crossroad, 1989.

Hickman, Hoyt L., et al. *Handbook of the Christian Year.* Nashville: Abingdon Press, 1986.

Lutheran Book of Worship. Minneapolis: Publishing House of the Evangelical Lutheran Church in America (first published 1978).

Sedgwick, Timothy. *Sacramental Ethics: Paschal Identity and the Christian Life.* Philadelphia: Fortress, 1987.

Thompson, Bard. *Liturgies of the Western Church.* Philadelphia: Fortress, 1982.

The United Methodist Book of Worship. Nashville: The United Methodist Publishing House, 1992.

The United Methodist Hymnal: Book of United Methodist Worship. Nashville: The United Methodist Publishing House, 1989.

White, James F. *Introduction to Christian Worship.* Nashville: Abingdon Press, 1980.

Willimon, William. *The Service of God.* Nashville: Abingdon Press, 1983.

Wogaman, J. Philip. *Making Moral Decisions.* Nashville: Abingdon Press, 1990.

CHAPTER SEVEN

Strategies for Christians at Work

I N THE LAST CHAPTER, we addressed the practical challenge of strengthening the connection between faith and work within our communities of faith—local congregations. In this chapter, we move beyond the walls of the gathered Christian community to consider how the individual Christian can live one's faith and Christian ethic in the workplace. If the local church provides its own peculiar stumbling blocks and challenges (as well as unique opportunities) to linking faith and work, so does the modern work organization. Let's look first at some reasons ethics can be a neglected or difficult topic within the cultures of work organizations and some stumbling blocks to effective moral action there. Then we can explore strategic and practical suggestions for putting faith to work within organizations.

To offer strategies for Christians at work is to presume that ethics generally have a legitimate place within work organizations and that Christians can and should bring religious values into secular roles and workplaces. For some, though, such connection may be considered difficult at best, and perhaps even impossible. Some might claim that the capitalist imperative to generate profits in a competitive marketplace encourages and nurtures values and qualities of character (such as greed, acquisitiveness, and competitiveness) that are radically inconsistent with Christian values and qualities of character (such as self-sacrifice and cooperation).

Should Christians be expected to bring Christian ethical values with us into work roles and work organizations? Or is it okay for us to check them at the door and take on another set of values for work? We must assert the former if we believe in the sovereignty of God over all realms of life, including the economy. Even so, it is by no means always easy and clear to determine *what* Christian ethical values we ought to bring with us and *how* we ought to apply them. Adding to this ambiguity is the uncertainty of what to expect ethically from business corporations in modern Western societies. As Max Stackhouse has argued, "The problem is that we do not quite know how to assess what we have ethically" ("The Moral Roots of the Corporation").

STUMBLING BLOCKS AND CHALLENGES TO EFFECTIVE ETHICAL ACTION AT WORK

Ethics at work—living out the ethical values we hold as central to our lives; engaging in moral reflection, debate, and decision making with others in the organization; working within and shaping the ethical character of our corporate cultures—can be challenging and exciting at best, and frustrating and fraught with stumbling blocks at worst. Let's briefly consider some common stumbling blocks.

1. *We may assume that ethical considerations, whether informed by religious faith or not, have little or no legitimate place within a competitive business organization driven by the need to generate profits to survive.* Perhaps we feel that external constraints bearing down on a business are so hostile as to leave no moral breathing space for us to make ethical choices within our organizations. For instance, industry consolidation and fierce global competition are forcing some organizations to desperately slash production costs, including wages and jobs, to survive. Perhaps we are concerned ethically about the emotional pain that dislocated

workers suffer and think it is wrong to lay off workers in ways that place inordinate burdens on them. Yet we justify the layoff decision as an unavoidable response to an external condition. George Bremer often feels this unavoidability. Jane Corey rejects this unavoidability, believing that corporate managements have more moral breathing space and discretionary power to protect workers than George Bremer sometimes feels.

2. *We observe that the culture of the organization discourages certain kinds of ethical action and deliberation.* Corporate cultures can vary dramatically from organization to organization. They include policies, rules, formal procedures, and informal patterns and styles of action and behavior that tell us what is appropriate behavior and what is not. All corporate cultures provide guidelines and clues for determining which questions and issues are considered acceptable to raise and which are not. Perhaps we perceive the organization's culture as closed, even to the point of being hostile and recriminatory to persons who raise certain issues or act in certain ways. For instance, some organizations have worked hard to develop cultures that discourage acts of sexual harassment and to make it easier for workers to disclose and investigate alleged cases of sexual harassment, free from fear of recrimination. Others have not, making it extremely painful and difficult for victims to bring such actions to the light of effective investigation and organizational response.

3. *We may feel that doing the right thing or addressing an ethical issue courageously may involve substantial personal risk to our positions, reputations, and future prospects within our organizations or careers.* As every organization has its own unique culture, so every organization has its own politics. Sometimes office politics can be destructive of trust, productivity, and morale. Persons with authority sometimes wield power in unfair, dishonest, mean-spirited, discriminatory, or inordi-

nately self-serving ways. Within such cultures, we may feel at grave personal risk in doing the right thing or raising an issue of ethical concern, even worried about the possibility of retribution or recrimination by others. For years, Barb Daniels has placed herself at personal risk by raising issues of racism and exclusion within her organization, and she has developed great personal courage in the process.

4. *We may lack power, authority, or support to make a decision that we think is ethically appropriate, to correct a practice that we think is wrong or harmful, or to institute a change in policy or corporate culture that we think would create ethical improvement in the organization.* Such constraints are a fact of life for any person in any organization, even the CEO. We operate within our spheres of influence, some very narrow, some larger. Few changes, even ethical ones, can be made unilaterally. Changes usually require persuasion, consensus, and the support of others who also will be affected. The challenge for every worker is to determine which battles to fight and which to leave for another day. And when we identify the issues we wish to tackle, we are faced with the strategic and prudential questions of determining the best ways to achieve our desired outcomes.

5. *The organization may lack institutional clarity about the ethical expectations and standards for its people.* In the absence of clearly understood norms and expectations, even well-intentioned people can make inappropriate or poor ethical choices in ambiguous or fuzzy situations. Furthermore, in an increasingly pluralistic society, it may be too much to expect that the individuals in our workforce come with the same set of ethical standards about how to conduct themselves in the workplace. Organizations that fail to intentionally and explicitly clarify the ethical standards they want to pervade their cultures and practices run the risk of workers' ethical lapses. Mission statements, ethics and value statements, and ethics training can become effective

ways for organizations to communicate ethical expectations and standards for workers.

6. *We may feel uncertain about how far and through what means to carry the ethical convictions and norms of our faith into a secular workplace.* As we discussed in chapter 4, we are challenged by translating the norms and beliefs of theology and faith into language accessible to others, especially in communities and situations that are outside the walls of the Christian community. Sometimes we may not wish to wear our Christianity on our sleeves, at least in the sense of always using explicitly religious language in secular settings. Most of us would agree that there are inappropriate ways to communicate faith commitments within settings such as the workplace. For example, hiring only individuals who espouse a particular religious faith would be inappropriate. Using explicitly biblical language and concepts in business meetings among persons with widely divergent faith commitments, including those with no explicit religious orientation, might be overbearing. People rarely wish to be preached to. Instead, we may need to find common ethical concepts that can be justified by appeal to a variety of languages, religious and nonreligious, such as justice and fairness. We may wish to embody our Christian ethical values "silently," through our actions, character traits, and patterns of behavior rather than through our words.

Organizational obstacles can be real and sometimes feel intractable. They can make doing Christian ethics at work complex, sometimes ambiguous, and even frustrating and painful. Each can limit our effectiveness. Together, they are the pressure points where we can feel the rub between our faith and our work. They define the contours of some of our challenges and can affect our successes and failures in keeping faith at work.

THE PURPOSE OF BUSINESS AND AN ORGANIZATION'S MISSION

Let me suggest a place to begin thinking in a more focused way about how to relate our faith more effectively to our work. Let's step back and ask a very broad question: What is the fundamental purpose of business today? To clarify its purpose helps us to judge its worth or value in modern society and to define our roles and expectations as workers. The importance of this question is heightened by the fact that the modern corporation, especially the business corporation, may be *the* most distinctive and defining feature of modern social life, perhaps more significant than the family, the state, and voluntary organizations such as the church.

In this short space, I cannot propose and defend a single answer to the question of the fundamental purpose of business organizations today. The question is deep and profound, and there are many possible answers in a changing, pluralistic society. Is the basic role merely one of economic efficiency—to expand production? Is it solely to maximize return on equity for shareholders? Is it fundamentally to provide employment for a nation's people? Is it to provide the highest quality goods and services for customers? Is it to generate economic wealth for a society? In his recent papal encyclical, *Centesimus Annus,* John Paul II proposes the following answer:

> The purpose of a business firm is not simply to make a profit, but is to be found in its very existence as a community of persons who in various ways are endeavoring to satisfy their basic needs, and who form a particular group at the service of the whole of society. Profit is a regulator of the life of a business, but it is not the only one; other human and moral factors must also be considered which, in the long term, are at least equally important for the life of a business.

148

I invite you to articulate your provisional response to the question, informed by your own Christian perspective on the world. How we think and act within our economic organizations depends in part on what we view as their primary purposes. Max Stackhouse asserts that the chief, distinctive purpose of the economic corporation is to increase wealth; he also argues that the moral core of the corporation is not in economics or in its relative efficiencies, but in its ethos, whose historical roots in Western civilization are deeply moral and spiritual. In its fullest sense, the business corporation's purpose cannot be defined *only* in terms of its instrumental value in the production and distribution of goods and services. It must also be viewed, as Robert Solomon claims, as an essential part of the good life and the good society.

Consider the purpose or mission of the organization for which you work. What is its basic purpose or mission? Does it have a clear sense of purpose or mission? If so, do its products or services, its internal practices, and its external relationships fit well with that sense of mission? Do its basic mission and the organizational values for achieving its mission resonate with your sense of self, including your Christian identity and values? Simply stated, do you believe ethically in what your organization does? Are its contributions to the world and its effects on the world ones that you affirm ethically? Is your work organization creating the kind of world that is consistent with the personal ethical worldview informed by your faith? No organization is perfect, nor is any individual worker. We ought not to expect moral perfection, but neither should we tolerate moral mediocrity from ourselves or our organizations. When the inconsistencies between our values and purposes and those of our organizations are severe, we can find ourselves in difficult, uncomfortable, even precarious situations.

If we wish to bridge this moral gap, we are faced with three possible choices. First, we might decide that our moral values and/or personal expectations of the organization are inappropriate and therefore try to modify them in favor of the values of the organization. Second, we might decide that the organization's values or practices are somehow inappropriate or inadequate and thus try to work toward the organization's reform, improvement, or transformation. Third, we might conclude that the moral gap is too large and intractable and as a result decide to leave the organization. The third option is always available and sometimes appropriate, but most of us will shun this option, except as a last resort.

CHRISTIAN ETHICS AT WORK: STRATEGIC PROPOSALS AND SUGGESTIONS

Having asked you to think broadly about the purpose of business in general, the mission and purpose of your work organization, and the values that motivate your work, let me offer some constructive proposals and suggestions for more effectively putting faith and ethics to work in your organization.

Create a personal mission statement for your work. In his highly acclaimed and insightful book, *The Seven Habits of Highly Effective People,* Stephen Covey urges each reader to create a personal mission statement. This short philosophical statement answers three questions: (1) what you want to be (character), (2) what you want to do (contributions and achievements), and (3) the core values and principles upon which such being and doing are based.

This exercise can easily be adapted to become a personal Christian ethical mission statement for your work life. First, what core Christian ethical values and principles (such as those outlined in chapter 2) are most compelling to you and can be the guiding concepts for your mission statement?

Christian faith offers an abundance of candidates: steward-ship, vocation, love, justice, the common good, and so on. Second, what character traits consistent with these Christian values do you want to demonstrate in your work decisions and actions? Examples might include honesty, compassion, fairness, and active support of peers or employees. Third, what occupational achievements and contributions do you want to accomplish based on these values and character traits? These can include choices about the kind of organi-zation for which to work, the profession or occupation that you want to hold, and the tasks and activities that you find most fulfilling and most wish to do. This statement might begin to look like a career planning and development exer-cise, but one that is directly related to your faith and is connected to your most deeply held spiritual values and commitments. In effect, this personal mission statement can be a summary of your Christian ethic at work.

Compare your personal mission statement to the mission and values of your organization. How does your sense of vocational purpose and ethical conviction compare to how your organi-zation understands its sense of mission, purpose, and values? Where the fit is relatively close, individuals tend to be highly effective and fulfilled workers. Where the gap is large, indi-vidual workers can be frustrated and their productivity can suffer. You can also feel the pull of conscience if your organization's ethical character diverges significantly from your own, especially if it causes you to tolerate actions and practices that you consider ethically wrong or questionable.

No organization is ethically perfect, nor is any individual participant. You ought not to expect perfection from your-self or your organization, but you can aim for moral integrity, improvement, and at least moderate and tolerable agree-ment between your values and the practices of your organi-zation. Gaps will always exist between your personal ethical aspirations and ideals, on the one hand, and the rough-and-tumble realities of practice and performance, on the other. Learning how to empower yourself and your organization to deal with and try to close the gaps becomes your primary strategic quest.

Identify potential and/or actual areas of ethical vulnerability within your work and within your organization. Virtually every job is vulnerable to unethical behaviors and practices and to less than ethically ideal decisions or actions. Try to identify these ethical issues and challenges within your position and within your sphere of influence at your workplace. Consider how you might intentionally and strategically address these issues constructively with the ethical resources of your faith.

Likewise, ethical problems, lapses of judgment, and unfair decisions and practices can occur in any organization, be it a large corporation, small business, government agency, or nonprofit organization. In an organization truly concerned about being ethically vigilant, management recognizes the areas that are vulnerable to abuse or ethical lapse, such as purchasing, sales, regulatory areas, and hiring, and attempts to strengthen these areas before problems occur.

Evaluate your organization's capacity for ethical responsiveness. Within the field of business ethics, experts have identified some key components that encourage high levels of ethical conduct within organizations. You may find it helpful to evaluate your organization in view of these elements.

1. A visible commitment to top managers, especially the chief executive officer. Organizational cultures are shaped by the person in charge more than anything else. For better or for worse, managements tend to reflect the substance and style of their leaders, be they large or small organizations. If ethics through leadership word and deed isn't perceived as important, it probably won't permeate the culture in any significant way.

This commitment is most effective when it is overt and clearly communicated. But it must be more than talk. If the

CEO pays lip service to the topic but is perceived as hypo-critical, talking ethics but not walking his or her talk in deeds can result in ethics being ridiculed and ignored by many employees. To quote J. Irwin Miller, the former chairman and CEO of Cummins Engine Company, "All of the corpo-rate standards of ethics don't mean anything unless the persons in the corporation perceive the top people to abide by them when the going is really tough." Ethics talk becomes pious platitudes when its principles cease to be applied in difficult situations involving real cost or potential sacrifice.

2. *A formal statement of values and ethical expectations, includ-ing clear policy guidance on difficult issues.* Ethics can mean different things to different people. Unless its meanings and applications are clarified and specified for each organiza-tion, talk of ethics can be virtually meaningless. Ethics can become a vacuous concept. Ethics documents often take the form of codes of conduct and/or conflict of interest state-ments that officers are usually required to sign on an annual basis stating that they have not knowingly violated prohibi-tions listed in the code. These documents are useful in communicating the message that certain narrowly defined activities such as conflicts of interest are strictly prohibited and can be punished. But they sometimes falsely communi-cate the notion that ethics is merely concerned with a narrow set of legalistic prohibitions—things to avoid doing with threat of punishment. Ethics can have a much broader and visionary role within organizations if we understand it to be the capacity to make good judgments as well as the virtues of character that make us good stewards of human and finan-cial resources. Also important are clear corporate policies that identify decisions and actions falling within acceptable ethical boundaries.

More organizations are developing statements of cor-porate ethics or values. These statements, often driven di-rectly from a corporate mission statement, articulate the basic principles, norms, and expectations that will guide policies and practices in a fundamental way. They can define general standards of excellence, commitment to clients and customers, and commitments to constituencies that should permeate an organization's entire culture. Such statements can be vital not only for large corporations but also for small organizations, including those where we know everyone who works there and where management styles are informal and nonbureaucratic.

3. An open culture that permits and encourages discussion of ethics and values. People within an organization need to feel they can address ethical issues with their peers and their superiors without fear of reprimand or retribution. Raising ethical questions does not necessarily mean that ethical lapses have occurred or that some individual, policy, or system is to blame for some negative outcome. Encouraging employees to feel free to raise ethical questions is the first step to addressing issues and potential problems adequately. The willingness of senior executives and managers to hear and act on the ethical concerns raised by responsible people within the organization is also critical. Only then will subordinates be convinced to take the risk to raise ethical questions in ambiguous situations. Ethical issues are resolved every day in organizations, either through open discussion and deliberation or through benign or malicious neglect.

4. Mechanisms to communicate an organization's ethics to all workers. Having a committed CEO and a formal statement of ethics or values may not be enough to guarantee the strongest levels of ethical conduct within an organization. Organizations that create ethics statements often must go the next step and create formal mechanisms such as education and training to communicate and interpret their values and ethical standards. Through compliance training or through the case study method, workers may gain practice in interpreting the meaning of values and norms for specific situations. General ethical norms do not always lead to clear application in specific situations. Rather, ambiguous situations require discernment and judgment.

5. *Mechanisms to monitor and reward ethical behavior, and to discourage unethical behavior.* Workers tend to acquire the habits and attributes and pursue the goals and objectives that are rewarded and reinforced through compensation, public recognition, and promotion. Ethics will be taken more seriously in organizations when managers identify ways to measure ethical behavior and reward it with tangible benefits. For instance, managers can be evaluated according to their capacities to attain diversity goals in hiring, retention, and promotion of their people.

Create support networks to nurture and sustain ethical character, deliberation, and courage. Business ethicist Michael Rion thinks that the single most important practical strategy for sustaining personal ethical identity at work may be to participate in small groups that enable regular sharing, support, study, and accountability. He argues that "what responsible managers most need to sustain those qualities of character so vital to ethical management, as well as to assess difficult questions of ethics, is an ongoing experience with a group that shares values and concerns" *(The Responsible Manager).* Such a group can be formed in various places—at church, in a professional organization, or in the workplace.

We explored in chapter 6 the possibilities for such groups to form within congregations for education and mutual support. At this point, I wish to emphasize the unique benefits of forming a support network *within* the work organization. Members of such a group may be extremely diverse in their religious and cultural backgrounds; at the same time they share important common ground by working in the same organization. What they may lack in shared religious understandings, they may gain in the ability to reflect on common ethical issues within the same organization. This shared context makes ethical reflection different from that in the local church. There, participants may hold similar religious commitments and common ethical values shaped by their faith, yet their ethical reflection on work is one step removed from the actual contexts within which they must put their faith to work. Here, in the workplace, participants benefit from the ability to reflect on a more similar set of work experiences. Here, group members may be more successful in identifying problems and issues, analyzing and thinking them through, and especially crafting solutions and responses that are realistic in terms of the persons, procedures, groups, cultural traits, and other structural dynamics involved in effective decision making and organizational change.

Such support groups are typically informal, outside an organization's formal structures, but not necessarily. They could be organized around specific ethical themes, such as how to deal with a diversity issue (e.g., gender, multiculturalism, sexual orientation) or how to deal with rapid rates of change and transformation (either structural changes inside the organization or external changes in the larger marketplace), or career development concerns (such as how to bring different generations of workers together for the mentoring and nurturing of younger workers). Such groups might be narrowly task focused and "change agent" oriented, with clear-cut organizational outcomes as their goal (for example, to make our organization more friendly to women and minority workers). Or they might not be so goal oriented but exist for the less-directed purpose of general, ongoing reflection, support, and nurture of members. The agenda for each meeting might consist of a specific problem or issue that one member brings to the group for their critical reflection, support, counsel, and strategic suggestions for resolution.

Confidentiality among members may be necessary, depending on the sensitivity of the information.

Michael Rion argues persuasively for the importance of such support groups, saying that ongoing communities are "essential to enabling individuals to sustain the courage and convictions necessary to carry on." He goes on to say that "the more a small community can develop sufficient trust among its members, the more likely that individuals will share their deeper concerns and take the risks that can lead to new insight and conviction" *(The Responsible Manager)*.

Create an organizational ethos that stimulates and enables strong ethical sensitivity, reasoning, and moral action. Encouraging and nurturing strong ethical decisions and actions among employees are important dimensions of the stewardship and leadership roles that managers can play within their organizations. How can this best be done? In their research on personal moral development, Thomas Lickona and Lawrence Kohlberg conclude that the following experiences and factors are most instrumental in the development and growth of ethical sensitivity, reasoning, and action for persons within groups:

- Being encouraged to see situations from various points of view,
- Engaging in logical thinking such as reasoned agreement,
- Having responsibility to make moral decisions,
- Being exposed to moral controversy,
- Being exposed to the arguments of people whose reasoning is at a "higher stage" than one's own (this assumes that moral development moves through discrete and measurable "stages," each of which permits a higher level of maturity in the ways that we make moral judgments),
- Participating in the creation and maintenance of a just community.

These experiences generally develop individuals into good managers—looking at situations from a variety of perspectives, logical thinking, taking responsibility for decisions, being exposed to managerial complexity and controversy, being exposed to senior managers with higher levels of experience and good judgment, creating and managing the rules, policies, and procedures that define the structure of work organizations. It should be no surprise that these factors and experiences can be optimized in developing high levels of organizational ethics as well.

Christians at work: return to the Christian community for support and nurture. Each of us participates in many communities. Our identities are shaped by the values of the communities and our roles in them. Often, separating and defining the many influences can be instructive. We move constantly among these communities of value on a weekly and even a daily basis—work, family and intimate relationships, friends, church, sports and leisure groups, civic associations. Through our participation in multiple groups, social values become interactive. The values of our faith communities affect our decisions and actions at work, and our Christian ethics inform our work and work organizations. The cultures, values, and practices of our work organizations affect the shape and development of the Christian community as well. For instance, within U.S. churches, decisions and group processes tend to reflect larger cultural influences. Most churches use *Robert's Rules of Order* to conduct meetings, a formalized set of rules originating out of a society that embraces democratic decision making. In any congregation, church meetings, informal styles of interaction, and even worship styles tend to reflect the styles and practices of subcultures within our society.

Work organizations do many things that can benefit society. One is the influence on surrounding cultural institutions, including the church. Work organizations are the bearers of social values as much as churches are. And at their best, work organizations become places where individuals can grow, develop, and flourish in ways they might not otherwise. Corporations can provide the conditions for the possibility of creative moral action in society. At their best, they can be vehicles through which Christians live to the glory of God and can be signs of divine grace in the world, permitting the possibility of individual and social renewal, regeneration, and transformation. Not to be idolized or confused with the kingdom of God, they are always less than this ideal. Christians at work, therefore, must be challenged continually to return to communities of faith in order to remain within the balance and tension of this interactive relationship of social values. We return to be renewed and constantly redefined and reshaped as members of the Body of Christ called to be workers in the world.

QUESTIONS FOR GROUP STUDY AND DISCUSSION

---

1. Do you face obstacles and stumbling blocks within your work organization that inhibit your effectiveness in living out your faith and ethics at work? If so, what are they? Are they insurmountable or subject to change? Which seem within your capacity to overcome or eliminate, and which do not?

2. What do you think is the primary purpose of business today? (If you are discussing this in a group, try to generate different responses and probe the implications of the differences for how we define our ethical expectations for businesses and for ourselves as workers.)

3. What are the mission, purpose, and values of the organization for which you work? Do they cohere well with your

personal values, especially those informed by Christian faith and ethics?

4. Which strategic proposals and suggestions do you find most helpful? How might you modify them better to fit your work situation and your organization's culture?

5. What additional suggestions can you offer for helping Christians to be more effective in putting Christian faith and ethics to work?

KEY RESOURCES

Business Roundable, The. *Corporate Ethics: A Prime Business Asset.* 1988.

Covey, Stephen R. *The Seven Habits of Highly Effective People: Restoring the Character Ethic.* New York: Simon & Schuster, 1989.

John Paul II. *Centesimus Annus* (papal encylical). 1991.

Kuhn, James W., and Donald W. Shriver, Jr. *Beyond Success: Corporations and Their Critics in the 1990s.* New York: Oxford University Press, 1991.

Rion, Michael. *The Responsible Manager: Practical Strategies for Ethical Decision Making.* San Francisco: Harper & Row, 1989.

Scott, Mary, and Howard Rothman. *Companies with a Conscience: Intimate Portraits of Twelve Firms That Make a Difference.* New York: Citadel, 1994.

Stackhouse, Max L. "The Moral Roots of the Corporation." *Theology & Public Policy* 5 (Summer 1993): 29-39.